Praise for Renewed

Heather Dixon knows firsthand the struggle to embrace difficult circumstances as she deals with an autoimmune disorder that has changed the landscape of her life. In *Renewed: Finding Hope When You Don't Like Your Story*, Heather helps us see Naomi in the Book of Ruth as a woman who didn't welcome the trials that continually came her way but who saw God working in the midst of them. This study connects us with the Book of Ruth in a unique way so that we can live with hope whether life's curveballs are for a season or a lifetime!

—**Melissa Spoelstra**, Bible study teacher and author of numerous Bible studies and books, including *The Names of God* and *Total Family Makeover*

Renewed takes a refreshing approach to the biblical narrative of Ruth. Through studying the narrative of Naomi, instead of her more famous daughter-in-law, Ruth, I now see the parts of my story I've lamented in the past with different eyes. You and I may never be loved by a Boaz. Bushels of food may be hard to come by in certain seasons of our lives. But, our God will restore and redeem our stories just as He did for Naomi. I claim this now, for Heather has helped me take some next steps of faith with a renewed sense of purpose and joy, even though my story is far from a painless one. In life's darkest moments, all I have is the only thing I've ever needed: the God of Naomi. And the same is true for you.

—**Tracy Steel**, speaker and author of *A Redesigned Life: Uncovering God's Purpose When Life Doesn't Go As Planned*

It's one thing to tell people how to envision a new life or to change their situation; it takes a completely different level of wisdom, heart, and compassion to guide people in living well a story that they never would have chosen. Heather Dixon, with her powerful ability to make Scripture sing into some of the darkest nights, helps women navigate those places where it can be hard to see God's purpose and presence. With a unique perspective on the story of Naomi from the Book of Ruth, Heather will help you learn to thrive in the situations and circumstances you didn't see coming. You'll be renewed in spirit, heart, hope, and purpose through these pages!

—**Julie Lyles Carr**, best-selling author, speaker, and host of the *AllMomDoes* podcast

HEATHER M. DIXON

RENEWED

FINDING HOPE WHEN YOU DON'T LIKE YOUR STORY

LESSONS FROM NAOMI IN THE BOOK OF RUTH

Abingdon Women/Nashville

Renewed

Finding Hope When You Don't Like Your Story

ISBN 978-1-7910-0617-4

20 21 22 23 24 25 26 27 28 29 — 10 9 8 7 6 5 4 3 2 1
MANUFACTURED IN THE UNITED STATES OF AMERICA

Contents

About the Author

Heather M. Dixon is an author, speaker, and Bible teacher who understands living with a story that is not easy. Diagnosed with an incurable and terminal genetic disorder that she inherited from her mother, she is passionate about encouraging and equipping women to trust in God, face their greatest fears, and live with hope, especially in the midst of difficult circumstances. When she is not blogging at The Rescued Letters or speaking at women's conferences and events, Heather loves to make the most of everyday moments such as cooking for her husband and son, brainstorming all the possible ways to organize Legos and superheroes, checking out way too many library books, or unashamedly indulging in her love for all things Disney. Heather is the author of *Determined: Living Like Jesus in Every Moment* and *Ready: Finding the Courage to Face the Unknown*, and she is a regular contributor to *Journey* magazine.

Follow Heather:

🐦 @rescuedletters

📷 @rescuedletters

f @rescuedletters

📌 @rescuedletters

Blog: TheRescuedLetters.com
(check here also for event dates and booking information)

Introduction

When was the last time you delighted in a good story? Maybe you stayed up all night reading a novel you couldn't put down. Or you curled up on the couch to watch an engaging movie. Perhaps a friend or a family member recounted a tale that captivated your attention.

Everyone loves a good story, and most of them follow the same template. Take, for example, the typical narrative story arc. First, we are introduced to the characters, setting, and basic details of the plotline ahead. Soon a conflict arises that must be resolved, usually with tension-inducing action, a climax, and a few final details to wrap up any loose ends. Finally, all good stories reach a resolution. If you are like me, your favorite stories are the ones with a happy ending.

But what about *your* story?

Each one of us is carrying a unique story. Imagine your life thus far, written on the tender pages of a leather-bound book. Where would your story begin? Consider the setting and the characters in detail. See the faces of your story in your mind: you as an infant, a child, a young adult, and now. See family and friends who have helped shaped who you are today. How did your story advance and change? Think about the pieces of your story that created tension and conflict. Think of the most life-altering moment you've experienced thus far. Was it what you expected out of life? Was it a story you would have chosen for yourself?

I'm guessing that, like me, your answer might be no. My life-altering moment was when I received an incurable diagnosis of the genetic, connective tissue disorder Vascular Ehlers-Danlos Syndrome. So far, this diagnosis has brought me a slew of major medical events, and it promises more to come. It is incurable. Unchangeable. Irreversible. It's a story that I do not like, nor would I have chosen it for myself. And yet, it is the story that I must carry.

Few things make us feel as helpless or paralyzed as living with a story that we don't like and can't change. Maybe you know that kind of story: one that involves the loss of a loved one, an unwanted transition, a difficult diagnosis, a dream that fell through, or something else altogether life-altering but nonetheless devastatingly permanent. We all walk through seasons of hardship that come and go, but what do we do if we are living in a story that we can't change?

There's a story in the Bible about that. The Book of Ruth may have been named for the leading character, but you might identify more with her mother-in-law, Naomi. Naomi understood what it felt like to live with an unchangeable story that hurts. Her life follows the general story arc we've already discussed, but it ends with hope. She does get that happy ending, even though the path to get there is marked with hardship.

Your story ends with hope too.

Over the next four weeks as we study the Book of Ruth together, we will step into Naomi's side of the story. If you've studied this book before, you might be familiar with Ruth's determination or Boaz's kindness. But I want us to walk a mile, or four weeks, in Naomi's shoes, because I think her story has something valuable to teach us. As we look at things from her perspective, I suspect you'll find that Naomi is one of us. She'd feel right at home sitting at the dinner table with us and sharing a meal as we all tried to find the courage to lift our chins and figure out where to go from here.

When my doctor delivered the news of my diagnosis, I thought my story was over. But here's the plot twist that I wasn't expecting, and it's true for both me and you: God renews our stories. That life-altering moment isn't the end. If we're courageous enough to trust God with our stories, it can be the beginning of a new hope rooted in His promise of redemption.

So, if you (or someone you love) are carrying a story you don't like, I invite you to walk through Naomi's story with me. Together, we'll learn to flourish as we live out our hard stories and trust that God can transform them. We'll trade our heartache for delight as we discover a God who rescues and redeems. We'll learn to rely on God's movement in the details of our story, even when we can't always see it. And we'll gain the confidence to take action on the parts of our story that we *can* change as we watch expectantly for God to redeem the parts that we *can't*.

Your story isn't over. Even now God is working to renew it.

Getting Started

As we dive into the Book of Ruth, we'll find the courage to live by faith and embrace renewed joy. Here's what you'll find within these pages:

Four weeks of study with three days of lessons each week. The most efficient way to hear the voice of God is to immerse yourself in His Word. To get the most out of this study, this is where you'll want to spend the bulk of your time in Scripture. Because we lead busy lives, this study is designed with just four weeks of study and three days of lessons each week. Each day's lesson will guide you through personal study of a passage from Ruth as well as application of what you've learned. The lessons are intended to be done individually, but I know that certain stages of life allow for certain levels of participation. This study is intentionally designed to offer a flexible but thorough plan to walk through the entire Book of Ruth. You may find that setting time aside on Mondays, Wednesdays, and Fridays to go through each lesson works best for your schedule. Or perhaps it may be better to work through them on the weekends. With God's guidance, only you can determine the schedule that best suits your season of life. Here's what you'll find in each lesson:

- **Setting the Scene.** At the beginning of each lesson, you'll find some introductory or background material for the day's Scripture text. With the exception of the first lesson, you'll also find the same three questions here each time, called "The Deeper Story":
  1. What does this passage tell us about the human characters in this particular narrative?

2. Does this passage tell us something about God? If so, what does it say?

3. Does this passage give us hints that God is at work? If so, what are they?

These questions are intended to remind us that God is the most important character in the story, and they will help you personally consider the text *before* our exploration together.

- **Extra Insights.** These are additional thoughts and comments in the margin to help you dive deeper into the cultural context or theological topic for a particular passage.

- **Group Session Guide.** Although you can do this study individually and reap benefits, it is designed to be done with a group for encouragement, support, and accountability. The Group Session Guides provide an outline for a 60-minute or 90-minute group session, including discussion questions, activities, prayer prompts, and notes for the video segment.

- **Leader Helps.** If you are the leader of your group, you'll find additional resources in this section at the back of the book. *You'll want to encourage your group members to complete the first week of lessons before your first group session.* The weekly video teaching complements and wraps up all that you have studied on your own throughout the week. Here's what you'll need:

  ◊ **A Bible, or access to one via the internet or smartphone app.** If you are wondering which translation might be best, my advice is to read the translation you are most comfortable with. The majority of Scriptures used throughout the lessons of this study come from the NIV translation.

  ◊ **A pen or pencil.** This might seem trivial, but sometimes a good writing utensil can make all the difference. Here's a fun fact about how I walk through Bible studies: I choose a pen with ink that matches the color of the cover of the study so that when I make notes in my Bible, I can connect them to my time in that particular study.

  ◊ **Access to the video teaching segments (optional).** The video teaching segments help to wrap up all you have studied personally throughout the lessons for each week.

One Final Word

Although I may not know the details of your personal story, I have carried it with me for months as I have researched, wrestled with, prayed over, and written this study. I've thought about what keeps you up at night, what keeps you from putting two feet on the floor in the morning, and what keeps you from walking with hope when you don't like your story. The most important thing I want you to remember as you turn the page is that God loves you and cares for you deeply. And I'm rooting for you, always.

Much Love,

Heather

Week 1

The Story You Don't Want

(Ruth 1)

The light shines in the darkness,
and the darkness has not overcome it.
(John 1:5)

I watched the night sky light up through my bedroom window as I glanced at the clock. Counted. And then cringed as the thunder made itself known. I should have been asleep, but the storms wouldn't allow it. They continued to roll through our small town, one after another all through the night. I fiddled with my pajama sleeve as I wondered what kind of damage might greet us when the sun rose.

The weather outside echoed the circumstances of my life at the moment. I was walking through a season that could have easily been characterized as stormy, threatening, and dangerous. There were no man-made answers for what I was facing, only a prescription from the doctor to prepare my bucket list and live my life well. Sometimes what you are up against can make you feel like you are walking into darkness. In those circumstances, you wonder how in the world you will find the light from here and if there is any hope left at all.

At last, I heard the automatic coffee maker start to brew, its steady drip signaling that it was time to get up and face the day. Breakfast was made and lunches were packed and off we went toward the carpool line. On our way, we surveyed the damage of scattered branches, smashed bushes, and even a few fallen trees. Although the sun had risen, the sky was still a dark gray. We parked outside my son's school and got ready to walk in.

"Look, Mom, the light is beating the dark!"

I followed his gaze to one corner of the sky, where a small beam of light was starting to break through the cloudy gloom. Even with most of the sky still covered in the darkness of lingering storms, it was impossible to miss the light, brilliant against the shadows. The truth of God's promises rushed into my heart as the corners of my mouth turned up in a thankful grin.

Even when it seems that the forces of darkness might overtake us, God still reigns. He is not asleep. He has not forgotten. His hope will shine through the darkness if we can just remember to look for it. The light of His redeeming love will always win; it will always beat the dark.

God's Word doesn't promise us that we won't carry challenging stories, but it does promise that we follow a resurrected King who has overcome the darkness. If we keep our eyes on Him as we move through difficult times, we'll train ourselves to look for His light that always beats the dark.

Like that storm, we begin our study in a setting that was rather bleak. But we'll end our time in the first chapter of Ruth with a promise of hope. As we witness the light peeking in to beat the dark in Naomi's story, my prayer for you this week is that you might shift your focus from the darkness of this world to the light of God.

Day 1: Longing for the Light

Scripture Focus

Ruth 1:1-5

I first fell in love with Scripture when I accepted Jesus as my personal Savior. I was twelve then, and by the time I got to high school, God had grown a deep appreciation in me for His Word. My high school English teacher, Mrs. Darling, was also my Sunday school teacher, so Monday through Friday I learned how to analyze words of classic literature, and on Sunday I learned how to analyze the words of God. I adored both.

I remember Mrs. Darling teaching our class about the use of contrast in literature. Authors use contrast to highlight notable differences between characters, settings, themes, or even emotions within a story.[1] Some recognizable examples might be Dr. Jekyll and Mr. Hyde, the country and the city, light versus dark, or the battle between good versus evil.

To find a story that perfectly illustrates the use of contrast, open your Bible and flip to the eighth book of the Old Testament. In a time that could easily be described as dark, the Book of Ruth glimmers with hope. This is Naomi's story.

Read Ruth 1:1-5, and answer the questions below.

When does Naomi's story take place? (v. 1)

What is happening in the land at the time?

We are given the names of six characters in this passage. What are they?

Extra Insight

The events set forth in the Book of Ruth likely occurred sometime between the thirteenth and the twelfth century BCE.[2] For historical context, Ramses II, one of Egypt's most famous pharaohs, was crowned in 1279 BCE.[3]

Setting the Scene

Now flip back to the seventh book of the Old Testament, the one just before Ruth. The Book of Judges details a period in Israel's history when *judges* ruled God's people, rather than a king. Briefly skim through the twenty-one chapters of Judges and you'll easily see that it is not a story of Israel's faithfulness to God. It is a story of rebellion and idolatry among God's chosen people. It's also a story of God's enduring love and forgiveness. The last verse of Judges gives us a good clue as to the setting in which we find ourselves at the beginning of Naomi's story.

Read Judges 21:25 and rewrite what it says word for word.

The days when the judges ruled were "marked by such practices as widespread idolatry, syncretism (mixing features of pagan religions with those of Israel's true faith), social injustice, social turmoil, intertribal rivalries, sexual immorality, and other indications of unfaithfulness."[4] See Judges 2:10-19 for an example of what this time period looked like. This is the beginning *setting* for Naomi's story. Now, let's get a good grasp of our characters.

Reread Ruth 1:1-5 and fill in the chart below with details about each character.

*Take note of the meaning of each character's Hebrew name below.[5] We'll return to the meanings of each character's name in the video teaching segment for this week, so you may want to flag this page for future reference.

Character	To whom is this character married?	Where is this character from?	This character's name in Hebrew means . . .
	Naomi		"my God is king"
Naomi		Bethlehem	"pleasant"
Mahlon	Ruth (see Ruth 4:10)		"sickly"
	Orpah	Bethlehem	"destruction"
Ruth	Mahlon		"friend"
	Kilion	Moab	"back of neck"

Now circle the characters in the chart on the preceeding page who are still living at the end of our reading for today.

Naomi and her family are from Bethlehem, but they moved to Moab because of a famine in their homeland. Naomi's husband, Elimelek, has died. Her two sons, Kilion and Mahlon, have died. She is left with her two daughters-in-law to face what lies ahead, which won't be easy. The major milestones in Naomi's life thus far, based on Ruth 1:1-5, are her birth in Bethlehem, her marriage to Elimelek, a famine in her homeland, a drastic move to an unknown land, the death of her husband, the marriage of her two sons to Moabite women, and then the death of her sons. *Famine* is a good word to describe this part of Naomi's story—not only famine of food but also famine of family, her loved ones, security, and her home.

What words would you use to describe the beginning of Naomi's story?

Do any of the words you just wrote apply to your story today? If so, write about that briefly.

The first five verses of Ruth may appear to be just stating the facts, but nothing in God's Word is there by accident, so let's look below the surface.

A Divine Setup

Actually, let's start by looking at an overview of the Bible because it's always good to orient ourselves with the *type* of book we are reading whenever we open up God's Word. The two major divisions of the Bible are the Old Testament and the New Testament, but from there the Bible can be divided even further into eight different genres of literary forms: law, history, wisdom, poetry, narrative, prophecy, the Gospels, and letters.[8] Each of these different types of biblical writings has something important to teach us about God and something valuable to learn about ourselves. The Book of Ruth falls under the *narrative* genre; the writings under this genre tell the story of "God at work in his creation and among his people."[9]

To help us understand the biblical narrative genre, we might benefit from going back to elementary school. When my son was in first grade, his favorite books were a part of the Magic Tree House fiction series. Over thirty books altogether, the Magic Tree House series[11] recounts the adventures of Jack and Annie, who travel through time and all over the world to teach children about important events in history, along with a few imaginary settings as well. Throughout the series, the main characters remain the same, even though each individual book tells a concise narrative from start to finish.

When we read from the narrative genre of the Bible, such as the Book of Ruth, we can think of a similar setup in our minds. The books belonging to this genre feature the same main character, God. But they span hundreds of years of events affecting His people, which means that the human characters in each story change. Not every human makes the right decision. Quite the opposite, actually, these sections of the Bible expose the flaws of humanity.

But that's the point.

Narratives in the Old Testament give us a clear image of how people followed—or more often, didn't follow—God's Law even as He advanced His plan for humanity's ultimate rescue in Jesus. He is always the main character, even when He isn't directly mentioned. God is the hero of the story.

As we read through Naomi's story, let's remember that God is the most important character in this narrative. It may help our understanding of the Book of Ruth to always think about three things:

1. What does this passage tell us about the human characters in this particular narrative?
2. Does this passage tell us something about God? If so, what does it say?
3. Does this passage give us hints that God is at work? If so, what are they?

You'll find these same questions in each lesson going forward, so we can always orient ourselves with these priorities as we are studying the Book of Ruth. With the exception of today's lesson, I have intentionally put the questions toward the beginning of the lesson in the "Setting the Stage" section so you can consider the text itself on your own *before* our exploration together. Before we go any further, go ahead and answer them now for today's lesson.

The Deeper Story
What does Ruth 1:1-5 tell us about the human characters in this particular narrative?

To consider what we might learn from these verses, let's return to the literary concept of contrast. It will become familiar as we move through the Book of Ruth.

Naomi faces a number of impossible scenarios. She is now a widow in a foreign land. She has buried both of her sons. With no one to provide for her and no heirs to offer future hope, the story that stands before her is tragic, destitute, and insurmountable. If Naomi were sitting at the table with us today, she would likely acknowledge that hers was a story that she didn't like at all. How would she provide for herself? Where would she live in a foreign land? Could she guarantee safety for herself? Would she find happiness again? Everything seemed impossible.

And yet, God is the God of the impossible.

Read the following verses and note what each one says about God:

Genesis 18:14a

Jeremiah 32:17

Matthew 19:26

Luke 1:37

Ephesians 3:20

Using the wisdom you just gleaned from these verses, what advice would you give to Naomi at this moment in her story?

The splitting of the Red Sea for Moses and the Israelites, the crossing of the Jordan for Joshua and the Promised Land seekers, the risen Savior on the third day after His crucifixion—the Bible is full of examples in which God accomplished the impossible. Naomi's story begins in a very dark setting. Many of the major milestones of her life thus far are tragic. But perhaps this is just the kind of scenario where God's light can shine through. It's a contrast that will allow His full glory to shine.

God is about to flex His muscles in Naomi's story. But without the contrast between the impossible and God's possible, she might not notice His movement. The same is often true of us. *Difficult stories can become setups for the display of divine strength.*

We wouldn't see the brilliant stars in the sky if we were standing in a brightly lit city. We wouldn't notice a lush field of lavender if the blossoms were green like the grass beneath. We wouldn't hear the tender pluck of a harp string if it were drowned out by the sound of a full symphony. Contrast is necessary to highlight notable differences, even the difference between hard stories and God's movement within them.

Your Story, His Glory

Here's my challenge for you today: Would you be bold enough to consider that God has allowed you to walk through a hard story knowing that His glory will be able to shine through you? If that question elicits a strong emotional response, let me assure you that it does for me as well. Reconciling the goodness of God with the reality of your hard story is not easy. We will talk about that more tomorrow.

For now, what's your story?

Using the space below, chart a timeline of the major milestones in your life thus far.

Birth   **Now**

Extra Insight

To fully grasp the gravity of Naomi's situation, we have to understand what it meant to be a widow in biblical times. Christopher Ash reminds us that "a woman without a husband or father may flourish in our culture. But not in theirs. . . . We cannot understand this drama without this non-negotiable given of their world: a woman devoid of the protection and provision of a man was in deep distress."[12]

Our hard stories can provide the perfect backdrop to display God's strength, if we are willing to trust Him with them.

Now take a few moments and describe the setting of your story. Is it dark, like Naomi's? Marked by tragedy? Which doors have been closed and which have been left open?

Describe the characters in your story. Who has helped shape who you are today?

What parts of your story do you not like?

What parts of your story feel impossible?

It might be that everything about our stories screams *this is impossible*! And yet, as we move forward in God's Word, we will discover that sometimes the dark helps us to recognize the light. Our hard stories can provide the perfect backdrop to display God's strength, if we are willing to trust Him with them.

Closing Prayer

Father, as I begin this journey, give me the courage to trust You with my hard story. Help me look for Your light even when my story feels painful, impossible, and dark. I don't like my story. Would You open my heart to see that my story can become a setup to display Your strength? Teach me to walk in Your will as I learn more about Your promises in Your Word. Amen.

Use the space below to add any extra insights or prayers of your own:

Today's Takeaway

Difficult stories can become setups for the display of divine strength.

Day 2: Permission to Grieve

Scripture Focus

Ruth 1:6-18

"Is this permanent?"

Slowly, I lifted my gaze from my stomach to the nurse sitting beside my hospital bed. The action prompted searing pain throughout my abdomen, which shouldn't have come as a surprise given that I had eighteen staples covering a six-inch vertical incision down my stomach. I know that is the exact number of staples because I just counted the scars still remaining.

"Yes," the nurse softly replied. "This is permanent."

The last thing I remembered, before a quick kiss from my husband and a hug from my aunt, was signing papers in an emergency room approving exploratory surgery. Two weeks later, I woke up from a coma wondering why everything hurt as the nurse waited patiently for me to get my bearings.

The exploratory surgery resulted in the partial removal of my colon and a temporary ileostomy, both of which helped save my life from septic shock caused by a ruptured colon. The nurse who greeted me upon awakening taught me proper care for my incision and ostomy bag, but her words proved to be the most valuable gift.

"You have permission to grieve. This is not how things should be. It's okay to acknowledge that this is awful and to mourn what has been lost. Take your time. But then, we have work to do."

Naomi's story today reminds us that it is okay to grieve our hard stories. But even in her grief, she points us to an unwavering truth.

Read Ruth 1:6-18, and answer the questions below.

Where are Naomi, Ruth, and Orpah at the beginning of this passage, and where do they decide to return to?

In verse 13, how does Naomi describe what has happened to her?

Which daughter-in-law determines to stay with Naomi?

Setting the Scene

Our reading from yesterday told us that Naomi's family had moved from Bethlehem to Moab because there had been a famine in the land of Judah. Before we dive into today's passage, let's look a little closer at some of the details about that move. Naomi and her family were Israelites—God's people. But to better understand Naomi's connection to the land of Judah, we have to understand Judah's importance to the Israelites.

To do that, we'll need to go all the way back to Genesis for just a moment.

Read Genesis 12:1-9 and note what it says about God's promises to Abram.

Genesis 12 details the call of Abram to leave his home country and travel to Canaan. In the passage, we learn of God's promises to Abram, which are formally known as the Abrahamic Covenant. The Abrahamic Covenant promises that through "Abraham and his seed, particularly through Isaac (and then through Israel and the Davidic line), all of God's promises for the human race will be realized."[13] But it wasn't just a promise for future glory. It was the guarantee of spiritual blessings in addition to a physical land for all Israelites in Canaan, the Promised Land for God's people. Biblical commentator Christopher Ash notes that "we cannot hope to understand this without both understanding and feeling the massive significance of a family's inheritance, their portion, share, or lot within the promised land. This plot of land was far more than a patch of farming ground. It carried with it a share of all the blessings of the covenant God made with Abraham. To have that inheritance meant to share in the blessings; to be deprived of it would result in the loss of those blessings."[14]

Yet Naomi's family made the decision to leave the Promised Land and journey to Moab to find food. A move to Moab, whose people were considered an enemy of Israel, was an interesting choice to make. Scholars disagree as to why Naomi's family chose Moab; but because the author of Ruth doesn't give us that answer,

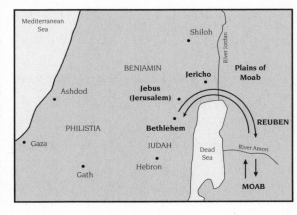

I rather like Adele Berlin's conclusion that Moab was the "closest territory to Bethlehem in which food was available."[15]

The Deeper Story

What does Ruth 1:6-18 tell us about the human characters in this particular narrative?

Does this passage tell us something about God? If so, what does it say?

Does this passage give us hints that God is at work? If so, what are they?

The Bitter Truth

When Naomi saw the events of her life unfolding, she called them "bitter." When you think about your story, particularly the parts of it you don't like, what thought patterns arise?

Read the following statements and put a check mark beside any that cross your mind as you consider your story:

_____ Life isn't fair.

_____ God is punishing me.

_____ I have no control over my life.

_____ God's promises are for everyone else, but not for me.

_____ I can only envision bad things in my future.

_____ God has no control over my story. My life is left to random chances.

_____ My story makes me sad, and I don't see an end in sight to my grief.

_____ I can't trust God with my story.

Extra Insight

The verb used in Ruth 1:6 to indicate that Naomi and her daughters-in-law prepared to go home is sometimes used in other areas of Scripture to signal action after the death of a person.[16] You can see examples of this in Genesis 23:3; Exodus 1:8; and Joshua 1:2.

While she is in Moab, Naomi hears whispers of the movement of God. There is food in the Promised Land, so she decides to return home.

_____ I cannot see how my story could get any better. There is no hope for me.

_____ God does not care about me.

Today's dialogue between Naomi and her daughters-in-law reveals that similar statements crossed Naomi's mind. Left to fend for herself in a foreign land after the death of her husband and her two sons, she is understandably distraught as she processes her grief.

Sometimes God puts people in our lives to help ease the weight of our emotional burdens.

Sometimes God puts people in our lives to help ease the weight of our emotional burdens. As Naomi decides to return home, both daughters-in-law initially agree to go with her.

> **Whom has God placed in your life to help you carry the burden of your story? Write their names here.**

The road from Moab back to Judah could have taken the women about a week to travel by foot.[17] Somewhere along the way, Naomi changes her mind about having Ruth and Orpah come with her.

> **Based on the conversation between Naomi and her daughters-in-law in verses 8-10, how would you describe their relationship?**

> **What specific words in verses 8-10 lead you to describe their relationship in this way?**

These verses imply that Naomi had an endearing relationship with both of her daughters-in-law. The tenderness between them is revealed in Naomi's expression of their kindness to her and to her sons. These women have considered each other family for ten years. Goodbyes are never easy, especially among those you care for. As difficult as it must have been, Naomi protests their accompanying her back to Judah.

> **Why might Naomi have encouraged Ruth and Orpah to return home?**

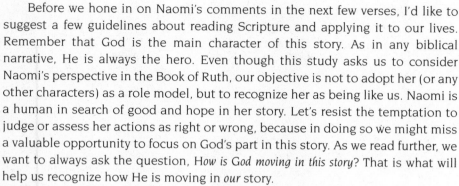

Before we hone in on Naomi's comments in the next few verses, I'd like to suggest a few guidelines about reading Scripture and applying it to our lives. Remember that God is the main character of this story. As in any biblical narrative, He is always the hero. Even though this study asks us to consider Naomi's perspective in the Book of Ruth, our objective is not to adopt her (or any other characters) as a role model, but to recognize her as being like us. Naomi is a human in search of good and hope in her story. Let's resist the temptation to judge or assess her actions as right or wrong, because in doing so we might miss a valuable opportunity to focus on God's part in this story. As we read further, we want to always ask the question, *How is God moving in this story*? That is what will help us recognize how He is moving in *our* story.

Now, as we consider Naomi's protests in Ruth 1:11-13, let's get a better understanding of the context in which she is saying them.

> **Read Deuteronomy 25:5-6 below. How might these verses apply to Naomi's situation?**

> *⁵If brothers are living together and one of them dies without a son, his widow must not marry outside the family. Her husband's brother shall take her and marry her and fulfill the duty of a brother-in-law to her. ⁶The first son she bears shall carry on the name of the dead brother so that his name will not be blotted out from Israel.*
>
> *(Deuteronomy 25:5-6)*

The Old Testament law provided for the care of widows in what was called a *levirate marriage*. About this custom, one source notes that "a brother was responsible to marry his deceased brother's wife in order to conceive a son and perpetuate his brother's name and inheritance."[18] Naomi references this marriage custom in verses 11-13 as she tries to dissuade Ruth and Orpah from staying with her, acknowledging that there is no hope for her to have more sons. Therefore, there would be no possibility for Ruth and Orpah to remain in and be provided by Elimelek's family.

However, Naomi recognizes that if they return to their families, Ruth and Orpah still have hope, even though it seems that her story does not.

> **In Ruth 1:13b in the margin, circle the word Naomi uses to describe her circumstances.**

Naomi has received criticism from some biblical scholars for the way she responds to her circumstances.[19] It can be easy to judge Naomi and assume her bitterness is evidence of a lack of faith, or that perhaps her priorities are

"No, my daughters. It is more bitter for me than for you, because the Lord's hand has turned against me!"

(Ruth 1:13b)

misplaced, or that her motives were rooted in survival instead of fellowship with God. But there are other scholars who affirm that her authentic expression of grief does not fall outside the boundaries of human faithfulness to God.[20]

What do you think? Was Naomi wrong to express her bitterness?

Perhaps, if we get into the habit of extending grace to Naomi, we might be more apt to extend it to ourselves. From Naomi's perspective, her story is over. Her husband and sons are gone. Without an heir, there is no possibility for her family bloodline to continue throughout history. What's more, there may be food in Bethlehem, but what will greet her when she gets there? As a widow, the odds are stacked against her. We can easily empathize with her feeling like there is no hope ahead. Before she can take another step along the road that will bring her home, perhaps she needed to express her emotional turmoil. The bitterness of her words acknowledges a raw and authentically human response to tragedy. Maybe she simply craved the space to grieve. Maybe you do too.

The precious nurse at my bedside was right.

You have permission to grieve.

You have permission to say of your story: this isn't the way it's supposed to be. It's okay to acknowledge that your story is hard. It's okay to mourn what has been lost.

But don't take that from me, or my nurse, or even Naomi. Consider these examples in which Jesus grieves.

Read the following passages and summarize how Jesus responds in each instance:

Matthew 14:1-13a

Matthew 26:38-39

Luke 19:41-42

John 11:33-36

Even Jesus, God Incarnate, acknowledged that life can be bitter. Jesus grieved. In exploring how grief is evidence for God, writer Sharon Dirckx notes that "if God exists, our sense of loss doesn't need to be suppressed. Grief is

It's okay to acknowledge that your story is hard. It's okay to mourn what has been lost.

an expression of injustice."[21] In other words, grief is our way of expressing the injustice we feel when things cause us pain or are not as we think they should be. It's also an acknowledgment that this world is broken and in need of Jesus. Naomi does not suppress her sense of loss, and by grieving, she points us toward God's existence and ultimate sovereignty. The bitter truth is that things aren't the way they should be. We live in a fallen world, and that truth pervades our stories. The world we live in isn't the perfect place God created at the beginning of time.

And yet, God is still all-powerful. And He promises to make all things new:

He who was seated on the throne said, "I am making everything new!" Then he said, "Write this down, for these words are trustworthy and true."

(Revelation 21:5)

This is a promise we can cling to in our loss. I can't tell you why God has allowed you or a loved one to carry this hard story. But I can tell you that our sovereign, all-powerful God will use it to bring about His purposes on the earth (Romans 8:28).

On Grieving Well

Let's take another look at Naomi's expression of grief.

Read Ruth 1:13b again in the margin. This time circle who Naomi acknowledges as responsible for her circumstances.

Is Naomi blaming God for her sorrow? Some scholars say yes.[22] Some scholars say no.[23] It's my inclination to believe that instead of placing blame, she was acknowledging a fundamental truth about God's character: His sovereignty. Sovereignty is the "biblical teaching that God possesses all power and is the ruler of all things."[24] Though God is not the author of evil (Deuteronomy 32:4), Naomi acknowledges that the Lord is still in control and He is still good, even when things hurt. Her acknowledgment points us to the hero of this story and ours, our heavenly Father. We can cling to the unwavering character of God even when our story hurts.

We can believe in God's sovereignty and still grieve our story.

In the summer of 1997, I was sitting in a quaint mountain church in Hendersonville, North Carolina, when I heard a preacher's statement that forever changed the way I viewed God's sovereignty.

I confess and regret that I am not able to give the preacher proper attribution. I have no recollection of his name, the name of the actual church I was visiting that day, or the specific words that he used in that statement. But the gist of his message was this:

If God is all-powerful (and He is), then everything in the universe is either ordained or allowed by God.

"No, my daughters. It is more bitter for me than for you, because the Lord's hand has turned against me!"

(Ruth 1:13b)

Ordained means God is the source or cause of something. Allowed means God is not the source or cause of something, but He neither prevents nor stops it from happening. This is a beautiful truth to delight in when our stories are easy. But what about when they are hard? What about when we walk through the unchangeable? Letting these words roll off our tongues becomes quite difficult when we don't like our story.

What feelings arise when you consider God's sovereignty over your story?

We can grieve our hard stories while still believing in God's goodness and trusting God's sovereignty.

I think about God's sovereignty when I consider my diagnosis. Did God *allow* or *ordain* my genetic makeup to mutate? Did God *allow* or *ordain* your hard story? I believe Scripture shows us that our loving God allows pain and suffering but does not originate or ordain it. Part of the purpose of this study is to help us get comfortable with this answer and unpack it. I suspect both you and I have, on more than one occasion, wondered why God would allow our hard story. We'll explore this in more depth tomorrow, but for now let's just briefly identify the good news about God's sovereignty. Here are three truths we see in Scripture:

1. God Provides—Ruth 1:6

And my God will meet all your needs according to the riches of his glory in Christ Jesus.

(*Philippians* 4:19)

The knowledge that there is food in Bethlehem, and that Naomi hears of it, is evidence that God provides for His children. He will provide for you, too.

2. God Cares—Ruth 1:8-9

He defends the cause of the fatherless and the widow, and loves the foreigner residing among you, giving them food and clothing.

(*Deuteronomy* 10:18)

God does not pay attention to a select few while ignoring others. He sees Naomi's story. He cares for her and the vulnerable situation she has found herself in. He cares for you too.

3. God Is in Control—Ruth 1:13

¹¹ Yours, Lord, is the greatness and the power
and the glory and the majesty and the splendor,
for everything in heaven and earth is yours.

> Yours, LORD, is the kingdom;
>   you are exalted as head over all.
> ¹² Wealth and honor come from you;
>   you are the ruler of all things.
> In your hands are strength and power
>   to exalt and give strength to all.
>   (1 Chronicles 29:11-12)

God is ultimately in control of Naomi's story. Even when all seems hopeless, He still reigns and He is still good. If He was in control when Naomi's life turned bitter (and He was), then He will be in control when it turns sweet. He is in control of your story too. Even though He doesn't show you the whole plot from beginning to end.

We can grieve our hard stories while still believing in God's goodness and trusting God's sovereignty. Take your time acknowledging the bitter truth of your story to Him today. And then whisper the truths about His character to yourself: God will provide for me. God cares for me. God is in control of my story.

Closing Prayer

Father, help me find the freedom to grieve my story. Listen to my honest heart about the things I have lost. I know my grief is an acknowledgement of injustice in this world. It's also an acknowledgement that, despite the sin and suffering in this world, You are still in control and You will remain in control. Let the knowledge of Your sovereignty and Your goodness bring me peace today. I trust You to provide for and care for me. Amen.

Use the space below to add any extra insights and prayers of your own:

Today's Takeaway

We can believe in God's sovereignty and still grieve our story.

Day 3: Following God to the Harvest

Slowly and methodically, I walked back and forth from the bedroom to the kitchen. As I turned the corner to change directions, I made a mental note that I was on lap thirty-three. I was trying to make it to fifty laps before I stopped to

Scripture Focus

Ruth 1:19-22

---

¹⁹*So the two women went on until they came to Bethlehem. When they arrived in Bethlehem, the whole town was stirred because of them, and the women exclaimed, "Can this be Naomi?"*

²⁰*"Don't call me Naomi," she told them. "Call me Mara, because the Almighty has made my life very bitter.* ²¹*I went away full, but the* LORD *has brought me back empty. Why call me Naomi? The* LORD *has afflicted me; the Almighty has brought misfortune upon me."*

²²*So Naomi returned from Moab accompanied by Ruth the Moabite, her daughter-in-law, arriving in Bethlehem as the barley harvest was beginning.*
(Ruth 1:19-22)

rest. All in all, I would have walked a quarter of a mile by the time I finished. That doesn't seem like a long distance now, but back then it felt like a marathon. I put one foot in front of the other and tucked my left hand into the pocket of my bathrobe.

I was walking laps in my house that day as a part of the recovery process from my abdominal surgery. It's a slow process, requiring you to start over from the beginning to regain physical strength and rebuild endurance. Having been through multiple surgeries before, my bedroom-to-kitchen track is a path I have walked often. I've always walked it with my left hand tucked into my pocket.

When I am faced with a situation where I am starting over from the beginning, I imagine my left hand tucked into God's right hand. It might sound silly, but the physical act of keeping my left hand in my pocket reminds me of God's promise in Isaiah 41:10 to strengthen and help me. Like the words in Isaiah, today's passage brings true comfort when we walk through something difficult. We don't have to start over alone. New circumstances might be overwhelming, but God promises to be with us. And as we will discover with Naomi today, He also promises hope on the horizon.

Read Ruth 1:19-22 (in the margin) and answer these questions below.

Where have the women arrived?

Naomi gives herself a new name. What is it?

What is just beginning as they return?

Setting the Scene

No doubt feeling weary from the weeklong journey out of Moab, Naomi and Ruth arrive in Bethlehem. There is a stir among the women of the town and rightly so—Naomi has been gone for at least ten years. Bethlehem was located in God's Promised Land for the Israelites. Exodus 3:8 describes the Promised Land as "a good and spacious land, a land flowing with milk and honey." Its value to the Israelites cannot be overstated. The town has significance to Naomi's story as well.

Look again at Ruth 1:19-22. How many times does the word *Bethlehem* appear in today's passage?

The use of repetition in Scripture is often a clue that there is a deeper meaning to be gleaned. An understanding of the literal meaning for the town name of Bethlehem will give us insight as to why the narrator might have included the word several times. The Hebrew word *Bethlehem* means "storehouse of bread."[25] Having originally left the *storehouse of bread* because there was a famine there, Naomi returns home to the *storehouse of bread* because she hears God is providing food for His people there. God, the gracious provider, will not let her needs go unmet.

The Deeper Story

What does Ruth 1:19-22 tell us about the human characters in this particular narrative?

Does this passage tell us something about God? If so, what does it say?

Does this passage give us hints that God is at work? If so, what are they?

Coming Home

On Day 1 of this week, we discussed the use of contrast in the Book of Ruth, and today we'll see that concept again. Naomi contrasts two things: her life when she left Bethlehem and her life when she returns.

How does Naomi describe the contrast between these two seasons of her life? (v. 21)

Have you ever felt a similar way about your story? Describe a season in your life that you might define as *full*.

Describe a season in your life that you might define as *empty*.

Naomi identifies a vast contrast between what once was and what is now—between full and empty. It shouldn't go unnoticed that the words she uses to describe her circumstances could also be used to describe the famine her family has escaped from. Her life was full when they left Bethlehem because of the famine. But her life is empty when they return home for food.

Maybe you and I can relate with her word choice. When things are going well in our lives—the family is happy, our jobs are stress-free and moving in the right direction, we have no financial burdens, and we are healthy physically and mentally—we might rightly describe those seasons of life as *full*.

Think back to the season in your life that you described above as full. Was it that way because of the tangible presence of good circumstances or because of its notable lack of hardship? Explain.

For Naomi, and for us as well, walking through tragedy can change our perspective. We may describe those seasons of life as empty because we feel empty inside. I can remember days when the abstract emotions of grief changed how I perceived the world. Food didn't taste as savory as it used to. Music didn't bring joy in the way it once had before. Activities I once enjoyed were not as satisfying.

I wonder if Naomi might have had the same experiences. In fact, Naomi expresses such deep bereavement that she gives herself a new name. Naomi tells the women of Bethlehem to stop calling her Naomi, which means pleasant.[26] They are to call her Mara instead. The new name was not chosen randomly. In the Hebrew language, *Mara* means bitter.[27]

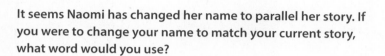

To get a better sense of the meaning, let's look at another place in Scripture where we find the same word.

Read Exodus 15:22-24 and describe how this passage indicates bitterness.

It seems Naomi has changed her name to parallel her story. If you were to change your name to match your current story, what word would you use?

Yesterday, I suggested that you and I might wonder why God would allow our hard story. Naomi's comments in today's reading take us deeper into this question. Naomi's story doesn't give us a direct answer as to why tragedy has befallen her family, but we know hardship and suffering on earth are a result of sin, and thereby evil, entering the world. Why does God still allow it? When we don't have clear answers from Scripture, we can always look to God's character for more understanding.

Read the following verses and summarize what each tells us about God's attitude toward evil:

Habakkuk 1:13

James 1:13

1 Peter 1:15-16

This small sampling of verses reveals that God does not tolerate evil. Although He continues to allow it until Jesus returns, His plan to defeat it has already been put in place. You may have an easy familiarity with John 3:16, but it declares God's ultimate answer to the problem of evil.

Read John 3:16 below out loud slowly and word for word. Then circle the emotion that motivated God's plan to give His one and only Son so that we might have eternal life.

For God so loved the world that he gave his one and only Son, that whoever believes in him shall not perish but have eternal life.

(John 3:16)

Love. God's love for us motivates all that He does. He loved Naomi. He loves you. He loved us enough to enact a plan to save the entire world through the sacrifice of His beloved Son, Jesus Christ. I wish I could tell you that I have trusted in God's love throughout all of my hard stories. But like Naomi, I walked through a season of bitterness as well.

When I was thirty-one, my father died suddenly, and I didn't handle it well. Bitter and broken from his death, I didn't open the pages of God's Word for about four years. Blaming God for bringing misfortune upon me, I turned away from God, Jesus, and the church. Those were the darkest four years of my life.

But in a way that only Jesus could orchestrate, He lovingly and patiently wooed me back into a close and personal relationship with Him. It began on my back porch, before sunrise, as I dusted off the Bible my grandparents gave me when I was eleven. I turned the pages to remember the God who had never left my side, even though everything in this broken world tried to convince me otherwise. The holy words rushed back into my heart and washed over my pain. They changed me and I was rescued. This part of my hard story is why I teach the Bible today.

If you are reading this and you feel that there is no coming back from something you've done or experienced, I need you to know you are in good company. And I need you to know that Jesus is determined to love you, regardless of the choices you've made. I know this because this is a part of my story. It can be part of yours too.

According to Naomi, what has the Almighty brought upon her? (v. 21)

When considering your story, would you use Naomi's statement to describe it? Explain.

Earlier in today's lesson, we read from Exodus 15 to get a better understanding of Naomi's new name, Mara. God's people were grumbling to Moses because their drinking water was bitter. Let's continue reading to see what happened next:

> Then he cried out to the LORD, and the LORD showed him a tree; and he threw it into the waters, and the waters became sweet.
>
> (Exodus 15:25a NASB)

Beloved sister, do you believe God can make your bitter story sweet again? Would you be bold enough to cry out to God today? Hope is on the horizon. You might not know how or why or in what way God will make things sweet again, but you can trust that He is in control and is working for your good.

The moment our earthly circumstances announce that all is lost is the moment the heavenly seeds of hope are planted.

Hope on the Horizon

For Naomi, the heavenly seeds of hope are proof that the harvest is on the way. Just after Naomi announces her name change, we learn that she and Ruth are returning to Bethlehem as the barley harvest is beginning. This is no accident. This is evidence that God is at work.

Naomi's story began with *empty* bellies in a famine, and she describes her story as *empty* when she returns home. But as one source notes, the harvest "connotes abundance and plentitude, an antidote to Naomi's identity based in lack and loss."[28] Naomi is starting over, but there is hope on the horizon.

Isaiah 9:3 (margin) describes the attitude you might witness at the celebration of the harvest for the Israelites. Based on this verse, what might be awaiting Naomi as she returns to Bethlehem?

The harvest season is a joyful season of blessing and bounty, rooted in God's provision for His people. If you feel that your story has required you to start over, you can trust that, like Naomi, the seeds of hope have been planted for you.

As I think about my slow walks in the kitchen after surgery recovery, I remember it wasn't the only scenario that has required me to start over. I assumed new jobs, took on new volunteer roles at church, and moved to new cities. If you, like me, are not a fan of change, then starting over from the beginning can feel daunting. There are new things to learn, new relationships to build, and new routines to

You might not know how or why or in what way God will make things sweet again, but you can trust that He is in control and is working for your good.

You have enlarged the nation
and increased their joy;
they rejoice before you
as people rejoice at the harvest,
as warriors rejoice
when dividing the plunder.

(Isaiah 9:3)

Extra Insight

"The barley harvest began in late April or early May, the eighth month of the agricultural year. At that time, Israel brought the first fruits as a consecration of the harvest (Leviticus 23:10)."[29]

establish. It's much easier to stay in our comfort zones, but we aren't always given that choice. In fact, I've noticed that the rhythm of life is defined more often by change than it is by things that stay the same.

The beauty of relying on God every time we start over is that He can use it to build our spiritual endurance. Trusting Him to guide our steps along household laps looks a lot like trusting Him to guide our steps in a more challenging situation. We just have to remember to tuck our hand in His as we follow Him to the harvest.

Closing Prayer

Surely God is my help;
the Lord is the one who sustains me.
(Psalm 54:4)

Lord, let me remember Your promise to help me and strengthen me through all seasons of life. Remind me to trust in Your blessing, to look for the harvest, and to follow You home. Amen.

Use the space below to add any extra insights and prayers of your own:

The Story You Don't Want

(Ruth 1)

Welcome/Prayer/Icebreaker (5–10 minutes)

Welcome to Session 1 of *Renewed*! We are spending the next four weeks walking through the Book of Ruth, but we are reading it from Naomi's perspective. Our main goal for this study is to gain a deeper understanding of God's Word and to connect with Him on an intimate level. We'll also learn how God moves in Naomi's story as we glean truths about His character so that we can apply those same truths to our stories. Our time as a group will allow space to dive deeper into questions that arose as you worked through the lessons on your own. Today we will consider the details of the beginning of Naomi's story and how you define your own story.

Begin by opening up in prayer, and then take a few moments to share your favorite story that you have read or watched recently (any story).

Video (about 20 minutes)

Play the video segment for Week 1. Below you'll find an outline and space to jot down any notes or extra thoughts you may have while watching the video segment.

Video Notes—

Scriptures: Ruth 1:18-21; Psalm 16:6; Ruth 1:22; John 20:11-18; Psalm 139:15-16

The stories we don't want can skew our _____.

A return to Christ is the first step to _____ our story.

God can open and bless the most _____ of hearts.

Other Insights:

Group Discussion (20–25 minutes for a 60-minute session; 30–35 minutes for a 90-minute session)

Video Discussion

- Can you recall a time when your perspective on faith was altered because of your life circumstances? If so and you feel comfortable, share a few details about those circumstances with the group.
- During this time, how did your faith deepen, stay the same, or weaken?
- What are some tangible differences between a heart that is bitter and one that is filled with joy? Feel free to share either examples that you have personally experienced or examples you have observed in others.

Workbook Discussion

- So far, do you identify more with Ruth or with Naomi in this story? Why?
- What does Ruth 1 tell us about the human characters in this particular narrative?
- Does Ruth 1 tell us something about God? If so, what?
- Does Ruth 1 give us hints that God is at work? If so, what are they?
- What parts of your story do you not like (Day 1, page 18)?
- What parts of your story feel impossible (Day 1, page 18)?
- "Contrast is necessary to highlight notable differences, even the difference between hard stories and God's movement within them" (Day 1, page 17). Can you share a time when God's movement was especially evident in your life specifically because it happened during a season that felt dark?
- Consider the thought patterns from Day 2 (page 21–22). Which one resonates most with you today? What others would you like to share?
- Whom has God placed in your life to help you carry the burden of your story (Day 2, page 22)?
- How does the truth in John 3:16 provide the ultimate answer to the problem of evil (Day 3, page 32)?

Finding Hope (10–15 minutes)

Divide into groups of two or three and discuss the following:

- As you feel comfortable, share your hard story with the group. You can share some or all of what you wrote at the end of the lesson on Day 1 (page 18).
- How would you rename yourself to match your current story (Day 3, page 31)?
- How have the dark parts of your story helped you to see God's light?

Closing Prayer (5 minutes)

End your group time together by sharing any prayer requests within the group. You may nominate one person to pray for all requests or you may feel comfortable as a group having all members pray together. Ask God to remind you that there is hope on the horizon, even in the midst of a difficult story.

Week 2

The Movement You Can't See

(Ruth 2)

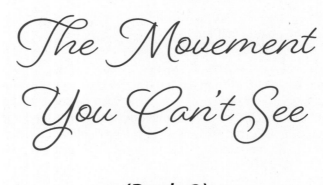

The LORD is close to the brokenhearted /
and saves those who are crushed in spirit.
(Psalm 34:18)

I had forgotten how much grief hurt. It had been nine years since I had lost a loved one, and the piercing sadness of it all took me by surprise this time. I left my mascara in the bathroom drawer for days, knowing that at any moment a wave of sorrow might come over me.

Grief has a way of changing our perspective. When you have lost someone dear, things that seemed simple before become an exercise in courage: putting two feet on the floor in the morning, making dinner, making phone calls, making our beds. Everyday occurrences can trigger precious memories of our loved ones when we least expect them. Grief hurts, and I was swiftly reminded of this when my grandmother died.

Although I had forgotten how much grief could hurt, I had not forgotten how sweet it could be. No, it wasn't sweet that I could no longer hear her voice or get lost in her hugs. I miss her terribly; there is no sweetness in that. But our days of mourning can be some of the most precious days simply because God is very near. As we walk through our grief, He is tender in ways that we might not otherwise see. God promises that He is close to the brokenhearted (Psalm 34:18).

In the days following my grandmother's passing, I began to notice the ways in which God was holding my family close. From her dear friends and former pastor who just happened to be in town during her last moments on earth; to the bluebirds that flew in and out of her bluebird house as we were planning her memorial service; to my Christmas cactuses, reminding me of her, blooming again; to the drops of rain that should have fallen during her burial but didn't....God was so near to us in our mourning.

Even more tangible is His Word spoken in Scripture; the pages of the Bible overflow with comfort and peace. So much so that some of the original language behind God's desire to comfort us paints a beautiful picture of Him wrapping an arm around us and drawing us close to His side (the Greek words *paraklésis*[1] and *parakaleó*[2] meaning to call to one's side, to encourage), even sighing with us as we sigh through our sadness (the Hebrew word *nacham*[3] meaning to sigh, to breathe loudly, to be sorry). You can see examples of these in 2 Corinthians 1:3-4 and Isaiah 40.

Whether you've lost a loved one or are grieving because of your hard story, I wish I could wrap you in a giant bear hug. You are not alone. Be tender with yourself. Seek God's voice in His Word and look for Him in your details this week. He longs to bring sweetness to your sadness.

Extra Insight   "*Paraklésis* carries the idea of bringing someone closely alongside in order to 'exhort,' 'urge,' 'encourage,' 'give joy,' and 'comfort' him or her....Jesus...spoke of the Holy Spirit as the 'Helper' or 'Comforter' (John 14:16, 26; 15:26), which is why the Holy Spirit is sometimes referred to as the 'Paraclete,' the One who comes alongside to exhort and encourage us."[4]

Day 1: Divinity Is in the Details

Scripture Focus

Ruth 2:1-3

After I graduated from walking laps in the kitchen, I ventured out on a slow and brief walk around my favorite park. As a former fitness instructor, I used to teach over eleven classes a week, but after my diagnosis changed my story, walking was one of the few options I had for physical activity. I walk daily, and the time spent pacing my neighborhood streets, the adjoining greenway, or the local park often turns into a prayer walk. I use the time to meditate on the Scripture I am reading and to pray for my loved ones, my ministry, and for those of you holding this book. But on this particular walk, I became especially aware of the many details along my path. I passed by a tree, split open by what looked like lightning; a scar in the shape of a heart was left in the tree trunk.

The tree told the story of what had happened the night before. An evening of heavy storms scattered leaves, branches, dirt, and broken flowers all around. But so many treasures lay waiting to be found in the midst of the debris, in the details. Even as the trees still carried the weight of the rain, the birds sang out, rejoicing after the storm.

Perhaps they knew what we are about to discover. God is always working in our details.

Read Ruth 2:1-3, and answer the questions below.

A new character is introduced to Naomi's story today. What is his name?

How is Boaz connected to Naomi?

In whose field does Ruth begin to pick up the leftover grain?

Setting the Scene

Naomi and Ruth return to Bethlehem, but now there is work to do. The two women are without a provider, a male relative to care for them, so they must find a way to feed themselves. In this week's reading, the action appears to shift away from Naomi to Ruth, but this is still Naomi's story. As Ruth so passionately declared in Ruth 1:16-17, the two women are joined forever. Everything that Ruth does affects Naomi. Ruth's plan to secure food is to go out and pick up leftover

grain from the harvesters in Bethlehem. Her plan is not without precedent in ancient Israel; we can find the first mention of it earlier in the Old Testament.

The Book of Leviticus includes some of the laws God gave to the Israelite people. Providing rules and examples of how to honor Him, God communicated them to Moses and Moses relayed them to the people.

Read Leviticus 19:9-10 and summarize this law in your own words.

Requiring landowners to not reap the edges of their fields during harvest and to intentionally leave leftover crops, this particular law provided for the poor, the needy, and the defenseless. It also provided for any foreigners in the land. Being from Moab, Ruth qualified as a foreigner.

The official term for the process of picking up leftover grain is *gleaning*. It was a good plan for Ruth and Naomi, but it's also a beautiful reminder that God cares for the vulnerable in society.

When the story we are carrying makes us feel vulnerable or needy, we can remember that God sees our needs and will make a way to provide for them. But something else is brewing in Naomi's story today and it's covered in the finger-print of God.

> **When the story we are carrying makes us feel vulnerable or needy, we can remember that God sees our needs and will make a way to provide for them.**

The Deeper Story
What does Ruth 2:1-3 tell us about the human characters in this particular narrative?
Does this passage tell us something about God? If so, what does it say?
Does this passage give us hints that God is at work? If so, what are they?

Code for: God Is on the Move

Oftentimes, we feel that God isn't moving, and if He is, He's definitely not moving fast enough. We cry out for resolution, quick action, or mercy in our

Extra Insight

The author of Ruth reminds us often that Ruth is from Moab. She would be considered a foreigner to the Israelites. For examples of Moab's history with the Israelites, see Genesis 19:30-38; Numbers 21:29; Numbers 22–25; Deuteronomy 23:3-6; and Judges 3:12-14.

prayers, and it seems those petitions remain unanswered. We wonder why, we wonder if God has heard us, or we suspect the worst—that maybe He doesn't care.

Given what we've already learned about Naomi, I imagine she felt abandoned as she arrived in Bethlehem. Why has God allowed this to happen to her? Has God heard her prayers for mercy? Does He care that this is her story? How long, O Lord, will she have to endure?

Today, we meet a new character in Naomi's story, and I can assure you he is not there by random chance; nor did he arrive too late. You've noted above that the new character in today's reading is Boaz and that he was a relative of Naomi's husband, Elimelek. This piece of knowledge is unknown yet to both Naomi and Ruth; we, as the readers, are given this exclusive information from the author.[5]

What other information does the author of Ruth give us about Boaz?

If the beginning of the barley harvest at the end of Ruth 1 was not enough of a clue that God was up to something good, these two new facts in Ruth 2:1 confirm that there is divine movement afoot. Not only is Boaz a relative of Naomi's, but he is also a man of standing, which can be translated as "a mighty man of valor."[6] Proverbs 31:23 gives us a good vision of what a man of standing might look like in ancient Israel:

> Her husband is respected at the city gate,
>   where he takes his seat among the elders of the land.
>   (Proverbs 31:23)

Why might the author of Ruth deem it important that we know Boaz is a *man of standing*?

Another man in the Old Testament is described in a similar way as Boaz. He happened to be both a shepherd and a warrior, and also quite talented with the harp.

Read 1 Samuel 16:18 and put a placeholder here for future reference. Note below who this verse is talking about.

Following the Israelite law set forth in Leviticus 19:9-10, Ruth sets out to pick up leftover grain in someone's field. Whose field, though? Consider the following description from Robert L. Hubbard Jr. as to how Ruth would have gone about selecting a field:

> Like fields elsewhere in the Near East, these were carefully apportioned sections of a large tract of land nearby. One individual might own several such pieces, which need not be adjacent. To take advantage of all available land, no visible fences or boundaries were used. Rather, each field was identified by the name of its owner. Such a patchwork of property, of course, left to chance the selection of the owner in whose field she would work.[7]

Each field was identified by the name of its owner, but remember that at this point, Ruth is unaware that Boaz is a relative of Naomi.

In Ruth 2:3b in the margin, circle the phrase at the beginning of the sentence.

Have you ever experienced a moment in which your circumstances appeared to be happenstance, but in hindsight you realized they had a divine origin?

As it turned out, she was working in a field belonging to Boaz, who was from the clan of Elimelek.

(Ruth 2:3b)

A few months before my official diagnosis of Vascular Ehlers-Danlos Syndrome, I had a lovely encounter with an emergency room nurse. I was there due to some intense abdominal pain, but we didn't know at the time that it was due to my genetic disorder. Why was the encounter with the emergency room nurse lovely? We talked about Jesus.

As if it weren't enough of a gift to simply have a beautiful conversation with a new friend, God had a deeper purpose in details of this conversation. Months would pass before my medical team would identify the true source of my abdominal pain. But not too long after they did, I just happened to connect with the nurse again. I told her of my recent diagnosis, to which her response was: "I knew God put us together for a reason. I have a friend with Ehlers-Danlos Syndrome. She would welcome talking with you if you would like."

To put this into perspective, Ehlers-Danlos Syndrome is rather rare. As *it turned out*, my ER nurse, who happens to love Jesus, also just happens to know a local friend with this disorder. At the time I met this nurse, I had never heard the words *Ehlers-Danlos Syndrome*, and we surely didn't expect anything like that to be the culprit of my pain. But God knew. And He was working in my details that day.

Do you have a similar story?

If you recall a moment where your circumstances appeared to be happenstance, but you later realized God was working in your details, take a few moments to jot the memory down here.

When we think God is uninvolved in our story, He is actually working in ways we would least expect.

The phrase you circled above in Ruth 2:3b is also not happenstance. *As it turned out* is used to "subtly indicate that God is orchestrating these events for the benefit of his people."[8] The phrase is a beautiful reminder that God is indeed sovereign. When we think God is uninvolved in our story, He is actually working in ways we would least expect. In a way that only God could arrange, Ruth just *happened* to find herself gleaning in the field of Naomi's relative. Already working in Naomi's details, God was shifting and moving things for Naomi's good. God is doing the same thing in your life too. *Your details are woven with divine movement, and God is always working for your good.*

Victory in Trust

We can't see the whole picture of our story. We don't have all the answers. But we don't need to. Knowing that God is actively moving and working in our details brings great hope. In the hardest of stories, God is moving in ways you may not even recognize at the moment. Suffering with health concerns? God is in your details. Reeling from a loved one's death? God is in your details. Struggling with financial burdens? God is in your details. Hurting from a broken marriage? God is in your details. Bitter with disappointment and shattered dreams? God is in your details. Concerned with a heavy decision? God is in your details.

Do you sense God moving in your details? Or do you find it difficult to perceive His presence? Explain.

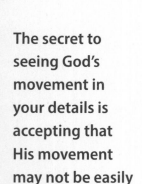

The secret to seeing God's movement in your details is accepting that His movement may not be easily recognizable.

The secret to seeing God's movement in your details is accepting that His movement may not be easily recognizable. Our heavenly Father, who is sovereign over all things, is working in ways that we may never see, so the posture we have to adopt is *trust*.

On a scale of 1–10, with 1 being the lowest and 10 being the highest, how would you rate your level of trust in God? Why?

Read Proverbs 3:5 (in the margin) and rewrite it in your own words below.

Trust in the LORD with all your heart
and lean not on your own understanding.
(Proverbs 3:5)

Four things happen when we trust that God is working in our details. Match the trust statement below with the appropriate verse by writing the correct number in the blank. Then circle the statement that resonates the most with you today.

A. God is glorified.

B. We are made to be like Him.

C. Our fears are extinguished when we trust in God.

D. The evil one loses.

_____ 1. *And we all, who with unveiled faces contemplate the Lord's glory, are being transformed into his image with ever-increasing glory, which comes from the Lord, who is the Spirit.*

(2 Corinthians 3:18)

_____ 2. *In addition to all this, take up the shield of faith, with which you can extinguish all the flaming arrows of the evil one.*

(Ephesians 6:16)

_____ 3. *When I am afraid, I put my trust in you.*
In God, whose word I praise—
in God I trust and am not afraid.
What can mere mortals do to me?

(Psalm 56:3-4)

_____ 4. *Then all your people will be righteous*
and they will possess the land forever.
They are the shoot I have planted,
he work of my hands,
for the display of my splendor.

(Isaiah 60:21)

Trusting in the Lord with all of our hearts and leaning not on our own understanding—this seems easy enough on paper, but trusting God is a daily decision. Start by looking anxiously and expectantly for Him in your details. Remind yourself in prayer of who God is, what He has done for the world, and what He has done for you. Give your entire heart to God, first in prayer, but also in your actions. If you think there might be pieces of your heart that you are still reluctant to hand over to Him, or you aren't sure what those pieces are, ask yourself: *What am I afraid of?* Our fears will always give us clues as to what we have not laid down at Jesus's feet.

God's movement is all around us. Let's trust that He is acting on our behalf today.

Closing Prayer

Father, let me remember Your presence in my hard story, not the story itself. Let me think back upon the difficult seasons You have already brought me through and praise Your faithfulness. Give me a mind that remembers You are always with me. And so are Your goodness and Your mercy. Give me a heart that recognizes Your presence in my details every day. You are with me in this story. You are working for my good. Amen.

Use the space below to add any extra insights and prayers of your own.

Today's Takeaway

Your details are woven with divine movement, and God is always working for your good.

Day 2: Wings of Refuge

Scripture Focus

Ruth 2:4-16

You may be able to pinpoint the exact moment things changed—the phone call you didn't expect, the doctor's appointment you didn't want to keep, or the funeral you didn't want to plan. Maybe yours is a story you were born with and you've never known a different way. But it's probably not difficult to determine the hardest part of living with a story you don't like. For me, it's the day-to-day obligation to put one foot in front of the other.

As you yearn for different circumstances you know will never come, you still have to do the work ahead of you. The dishes still have to be washed. The report at work still has to be turned in. The groceries still have to be cooked for dinner. Life goes on, even when life feels dreadfully unfair.

When you wish things were different, moving forward is a challenge. Today's lesson will remind us that we can put two feet on the floor in the morning. We can lift our chins with determination. We can keep going no matter what, because what lies ahead may be unavoidable, but what lies above is abounding in kindness.

> **Read Ruth 2:4-16, and answer the questions below.**
>
> **How does Boaz's foreman describe Ruth in verse 6?**
>
> **What does Boaz offer Ruth in verses 8-9?**
>
> **How does Boaz describe the God of Israel in verse 12?**

What lies ahead may be unavoidable, but what lies above is abounding in kindness.

Setting the Scene

The Lord be with you, today, beloved sister! Did that greeting make you smile? I hope so. It's a greeting filled with trust that the Lord is indeed with us and in our details as we move deeper into Naomi's story. And it's the exact greeting Boaz uses to meet his harvesters in today's reading.

> **How do the harvesters respond to Boaz? (v. 4)**
>
> **What does this type of greeting tell you about Boaz's relationship with God?**

We left Ruth yesterday in the field of Boaz, a relative of Naomi's husband. Today, we will see Boaz and Ruth meet each another in a beautiful exchange of generosity and grace. It can be tempting to romanticize their actions in today's passage. But as one commentator writes, "the character traits of Ruth and Boaz are ultimately a reflection of God, and this story is primarily intended as his revelation."[9] Let's keep that in mind as we dive deeper into today's passage. May the Lord be with us today, indeed.

What does Ruth 2:4-16 tell us about the human characters in this particular narrative?

Does this passage tell us something about God? If so, what does it say?

Does this passage give us hints that God is at work? If so, what are they?

Kindness That Heals

In the days when the judges ruled, kindness was rare. And yet, this story contrasts all that was dark in those days, and we find actions of abundant kindness throughout today's reading. I suspect you will agree that even though we are no longer in the days when the biblical judges ruled, kindness is a valuable commodity. Let's jump right in to identify every benevolent action.

Each verse from today's passage is listed separately here. Reread Ruth 2:4-16 and put a star beside each verse in which kindness was displayed. Next to each verse you star, describe the kind action(s).

Ruth 2:4

Ruth 2:5

Ruth 2:6

Ruth 2:7

Ruth 2:8

Ruth 2:9

Ruth 2:10

Ruth 2:11

Ruth 2:12

Ruth 2:13

Ruth 2:14

Ruth 2:15

Ruth 2:16

Are you overwhelmed with kindness yet? Boaz was incredibly kind to Ruth. Ruth was incredibly gracious to Boaz. Now is a good time to remind ourselves, as the author of Ruth is keen on doing as well, that Ruth, a Moabitess, is a foreigner to Boaz.

Does it surprise you that Boaz would be kind to Ruth? Why or why not?

What do you think prompted his kindness?

Let's consider what we know of Boaz's faith. His greeting to his harvesters gives us insight. We also know from yesterday that he is a *man of standing*. It is probably safe to assume that Boaz's kindness and his reputation are due to his deep faith in God. Commentator Christopher Ash says of Boaz's actions that "this man is to her a guardian, a protector, and a provider. He uses covenant language . . . to urge her to stay in his place of safety and plenty. He is to her a rock of refuge and living water."[10]

Sound familiar? We could say the same words about God's tender care toward us. Let's compare Boaz's kindness to the kindness of God.

Read the following verses about the kindness of God. Read them as if they were written directly to you, because they are. Circle the one that speaks to your heart the most today.

"But let the one who boasts boast about this:
that they have the understanding to know me,
that I am the LORD, who exercises kindness,
justice and righteousness on earth,
for in these I delight,"
declares the LORD.

(Jeremiah 9:24)

The LORD appeared to us in the past, saying:

"I have loved you with an everlasting love;
I have drawn you with unfailing kindness."

(Jeremiah 31:3)

Or do you show contempt for the riches of his kindness, forbearance and patience, not realizing that God's kindness is intended to lead you to repentance?

(Romans 2:4)

⁴But when the kindness and love of God our Savior appeared, ⁵he saved us, not because of righteous things we had done, but because of his mercy. He saved us through the washing of rebirth and renewal by the Holy Spirit.

(Titus 3:4-5)

Boaz shares the kindness of God, but more importantly, he points Ruth to the true source of kindness. In Ruth 2:12, Boaz tells Ruth she has come to take refuge under the wings of the God of Israel. The image is a significant one because it prompts us to remember God is gentle and compassionate with us. He does not withhold His kindness.

Choose three verses below to read. Beside each, write what function God's wings serve:

Psalm 17:8

Psalm 57:1

Psalm 61:4

Psalm 63:7

Psalm 91:4

Depending on which verses you chose, you just wrote a variation of the following traits of God:

- God's wings hide us and keep us from harm. (Psalm 17:8)
- God's wings provide mercy and refuge. (Psalm 57:1)
- God's wings offer a shelter of safety. (Psalm 61:4)
- Protection under God's wings gives us reason for joy. (Psalm 63:7)
- God's wings offer us armor and protection. (Psalm 91:4)

My personal favorite of the verses above is Psalm 91:4. I pray this psalm every day over my family, because I want all of us to uncompromisingly trust in God's faithfulness.

> **If you were to choose one of the verses on the previous page to pray over your loved ones, which one would you choose? Explain.**

One of the reasons I feel personally drawn to Psalm 91 is because it offers tangible comfort when I am navigating anxious thoughts. Anxiety often goes hand in hand with hard stories. When my story feels overwhelming, imagining God's wings of refuge and kindness brings great comfort.

On nights when I am particularly anxious and have trouble going to sleep, a prayer that utilizes God's gift of imagination often helps to settle my thoughts. I close my eyes and imagine a large field in front of me. Standing in the field are all the things bringing me anxiety, like current stressors in my life, confrontational moments, tension with loved ones, worry about the unknown ahead, or health concerns. Whatever is renting negative space in my head at the moment, I imagine those things standing in my field. Then I imagine a giant hand and forearm lowering down to the field from the sky. Slowly, but steadily, the forearm wipes all my worries on the field away. The field empties and the hand gently opens, revealing soft and gentle wings. I climb into them, curling up to rest in their protection as they fold over me.

When my story feels overwhelming, imagining God's wings of refuge and kindness brings great comfort.

In my imagination, the forearm, hand, and wings belong to God. I take several deep breaths and begin to meditate on the verses we read above about God's kindness and refuge. This simple prayer exercise helps me to remember that God's refuge and kindness are more powerful than my anxiety.

If today feels overwhelming for you, take a moment to pause and close your eyes. Inhale deeply as you imagine this prayer exercise, or create one of your own and write it down here.

The actions of Boaz in today's reading provide solutions to Ruth and Naomi's very real problems. In a culture that often rejected foreigners, Boaz welcomes Ruth with open arms. In a time when everyone did as they saw fit, Boaz offers Ruth much-needed protection. In a situation that threatened starvation for Ruth and Naomi, Boaz gives Ruth an abundant supply of food. His actions are tangible reflections of the kindness of God. *Heavenly kindness heals earthly hurts.*

Healing Together

Did you know acts of kindness extend far beyond simply soothing our anxiety? Scientific research has proven that acts of kindness increase self-esteem, energy, happiness, lifespan, and sense of pleasure while they lower pain, stress, anxiety, depression, and blood pressure.[11] Perhaps this is why Paul admonishes us to think on pure, lovely, and admirable things in Philippians 4:8. I love it when modern science catches up to biblical truth!

What are the current stressors in your life?

What details of your story bring you anxiety? Explain.

My challenge to you today is to meditate on the kindness of God. First, it will help ease any anxious thoughts stemming from living with a story you don't like. That may be all you can do for today. But when you are ready, ask God to reveal ways you can extend loving acts of kindness toward others.

Finally, brothers and sisters, whatever is true, whatever is noble, whatever is right, whatever is pure, whatever is lovely, whatever is admirable—if anything is excellent or praiseworthy—think about such things.

(Philippians 4:8)

People in your community need the kindness of God. Look a stranger in the eye today. When you do, I bet you'll see that you carry the same burdens. No, they won't have the same label, but we all live in the same broken world and we all carry broken hurts. We are not alone in our hard stories.

If we hurt together, we can heal together.

So be brave enough to look someone in the eye today *with kindness*. Maybe they are hurting too. And God might just need you to remind them also that kindness abounds as it flows from heaven above.

Closing Prayer

Father, help me remember today that You are kind. You are kind to me. You are kind to the world. You do not withhold your kindness from me. Let me find refuge in Your wings today and any day I am anxious and sorrowful because of my story. Then give me the courage to share Your kindness with those around me. I want to be a tangible expression of Your love to bring healing into the world. Thank You for Your unchanging loving kindness. Amen.

Use the space below to add any extra insights and prayers of your own.

Day 3: The Guardian Redeemer

One of my favorite places to visit is Walt Disney World. Yes, I am a total Disney nerd. I drink coffee from a selection of beloved princess mugs every morning. I can recognize most Disney movies by their font types. I often drift off to sleep listening to a playlist of instrumental Disney music. And I have a not-so-small collection of mouse ears to wear when we are in the happiest place on earth.

The one thing I talk about almost as much as Jesus is Disney. Some might call it an obsession, but I say it's a celebration of all things happy. When you live with a story you don't like, happy is a welcome feeling. And some of the happiest

If we hurt together, we can heal together.

Today's Takeaway

Heavenly kindness heals earthly hurts.

Scripture Focus

Ruth 2:17-23

feelings occur when my family travels to Walt Disney World. It's one of the few places where I can momentarily forget I live with an incurable disorder. The delicious anticipation of our visit is almost unbearable, but in a good way!

There is something about the anticipation of good things ahead that changes your perspective on the here and now. In today's reading, we'll feel Naomi's anticipation rising because there is good news ahead. And it promises to deliver more than just a momentary feeling of happiness.

Read Ruth 2:17-23 and answer the questions below.

How much barley does Ruth bring home to Naomi?

How does Naomi refer to Boaz in verse 20? What specific title does she give him?

What information are we given that might indicate Ruth would be unsafe in someone else's field? (v. 22)

Setting the Scene

We ended our time in the first chapter of Ruth with the knowledge that the barley harvest had just begun. We will end our time in the second chapter of Ruth today as both the wheat and barley harvests were finished.

True to Boaz's kind and generous nature that we discovered yesterday, he blesses Ruth with an abundant supply of the harvest. She brings home to Naomi an ephah of barley, which "could probably last the two women for more than a week."[12] This was a tremendous amount of food!

Can you recall a time when God surprised you with an abundant supply of something?

Whether it was intangible (joy, peace, wisdom) or tangible (food, money, material goods), how did it make you feel to receive more than you anticipated?

This celebratory tone is behind the words beginning our reading today—a surprisingly abundant supply of material goods Ruth and Naomi needed. God is the ultimate provider and He will always meet our needs. This amount of food was probably enough to make Naomi jump for joy. It would have certainly been enough to calm her fears about their need for food. But as we are about to see, God is just getting started.

God is the ultimate provider and He will always meet our needs.

The Deeper Story

What does Ruth 2:17-23 tell us about the human characters in this particular narrative?

Does this passage tell us something about God? If so, what does it say?

Does this passage give us hints that God is at work? If so, what are they?

The Go'el: A Glimmer of Hope

Naomi, who returned to Bethlehem *empty* is now abundantly *full* with plenty of food. This wasn't only an answer to prayer; this was also a manifestation of the character of God. God provides for the needs of His people.

Read Philippians 4:19 and Ephesians 3:20-21 in the margin.

How do the truths in these verses speak to Naomi's story today?

What areas of need are you aware of in your life this week?

Take a moment to pray Philippians 4:19 and Ephesians 3:20-21 over the areas of need you just jotted down. Write a prayer to

And my God will meet all your needs according to the riches of his glory in Christ Jesus.

(Philippians 4:19)

---

[20]Now to him who is able to do immeasurably more than all we ask or imagine, according to his power that is at work within us, [21]to him be glory in the church and in Christ Jesus throughout all generations, for ever and ever! Amen.

(Ephesians 3:20-21)

God below, acknowledging that you know He sees your needs and He will meet them, according to His glorious riches.

Understandably surprised by the amount of food Ruth has brought home, Naomi inquires about whose field Ruth has gleaned from. You and I already know it was Boaz's field, but Naomi is learning this news firsthand. To get an understanding of the fullness of her joy, let's go back to the first chapter of Ruth for a moment to recall a prayer Naomi uttered on behalf of her daughters-in-law.

Read Ruth 1:8 and write Naomi's prayer for Ruth and Orpah word for word here.

What does Naomi ask of the Lord toward her daughters-in-law?

Now, let's return to chapter 2 to take a look at Naomi's response to the news about Boaz.

What is Naomi's response regarding Boaz in the first half of Ruth 2:20?

This *was* an answer to prayer. Naomi prayed for the Lord to show Ruth and Orpah kindness. We saw in yesterday's lesson how God abundantly answered that prayer and today Naomi voices her acknowledgment and gratitude for God's faithfulness.

Then she adds an additional comment about the man who showed abundant kindness to Naomi and her family. If you are reading from the NIV translation, you'll see that Naomi calls Boaz a kinsman-redeemer or a guardian-redeemer. Other translations may use the phrase "nearest kin" (RSV), "family redeemer" (NLT), "close relative" (NKJV) or simply "redeemer" (ESV). The Hebrew word for each of these phrases is *go'el*.[13] Let's take a closer look as to what the word means.

Consider Exodus 6:6 and Exodus 15:13 below. I've underlined the English word that is translated from the Hebrew *go'el*. Based on the additional context within these verses, how would you define a go'el in your own words?

"Therefore, say to the Israelites: 'I am the Lord, and I will bring you out from under the yoke of the Egyptians. I will free you from being slaves to them, and I will <u>redeem</u> you with an outstretched arm and with mighty acts of judgment.'"
                    (Exodus 6:6, emphasis added)

"In your unfailing love you will lead
    the people you have <u>redeemed</u>.
In your strength you will guide them
    to your holy dwelling."
    (Exodus 15:13, emphasis added)

As one source notes, a guardian-redeemer has "an obligation to stand up for the justice of the dead or wronged person."[14]

Read the following passages and fill in the blank about what each one says about the obligation of a guardian-redeemer.

Leviticus 25:25-28

If an Israelite _____ his property out of necessity, the guardian-redeemer must buy it back for the family member.

Numbers 35:9-28

If a family member is _____, the "avenger" or nearest relative (guardian-redeemer) must avenge his death.

The guardian-redeemer is responsible for enacting justice on behalf of a deceased or wronged family member.[15] Now the light bulbs are turning on for Naomi. Boaz is related to Elimelek. He is their guardian-redeemer. He has an obligation to seek justice on behalf of Elimelek, and therefore he has an obligation to look out for Naomi and Ruth's needs.

Describe the emotions Naomi might have felt at this news.

Today's reading reveals another common literary device: foreshadowing. Through a guardian-redeemer, Naomi is guaranteed protection, provision, shelter, justice, and redemption for all that was lost in Elimelek's death. However, Naomi is not the only daughter of God who has rights to the benefits of a guardian-redeemer. This Old Testament story foreshadows the coming Redeemer in the New Testament—Jesus.

[7]In him we have redemption through his blood, the forgiveness of sins, in accordance with the riches of God's grace [8]that he lavished on us.
(Ephesians 1:7-8a)

Read Ephesians 1:7-8a in the margin. What are we entitled to through Jesus?

As believers in Jesus Christ, you and I are entitled to His promise for redemption—through forgiveness of our sins.

The biblical concept of redemption involves the payment of a "price in order to secure the release of something or someone. It connotes the idea of paying what is required in order to liberate from oppression, enslavement, or another type of binding obligation."[16]

When I accepted Jesus as my personal Savior, I understood His sacrifice on the cross paid the price for my sins. He redeemed me—bought my freedom—so I might have eternal life with Him. But His role as Redeemer didn't stop with salvation from sin. He redeems much more.

I gained a much deeper understanding of Jesus's role as my Redeemer when I began to carry the story I can't change. As I navigated the ramifications of my diagnosis and walked through multiple recoveries from major medical events, God made two things very clear to me:

1. There would be no confusion as to where my healing had come from. Because there is no cure or treatment for Vascular Ehlers-Danlos, God alone receives the glory for every breath I take.
2. The story I carry is just the gospel story made manifest. There is no cure for us except Jesus. While darkness threatens to consume, hope is found in Jesus alone. While humans say, "This is impossible," Jesus whispers, "All things are possible with Me." While this earth says, "There is no cure for you," Jesus says, "I am your cure. I am your hope. I can redeem anything and I will restore you completely."

Jesus doesn't just redeem our lives for eternity. He redeems our hard stories as well—though we have to be willing to let go of our expectations and agendas. *Jesus has the power to redeem both our souls and our stories if we surrender them to Him.*

Our Guardian-Redeemer

You may not be carrying a life-threatening medical condition, but all of our stories cry out for the Savior and His redeeming love. If you think your marriage is lost, Jesus can redeem it. If you have no idea how to restore a broken friendship, Jesus can redeem it. If you think you've made far too many mistakes to be rescued, I promise you, Jesus can redeem them all. If you are facing suffering and hardship that seem too difficult to face alone, Jesus longs to face them with you.

Jesus, our personal guardian-redeemer, redeems all things.

True to His gracious nature, He has taken one of the hardest seasons of my life and turned it into one of the sweetest. Every moment is precious. Every memory is priceless. By clinging to His grace, Jesus has given me a perspective that most people search their entire lives for—the appreciation of moments both ordinary and extraordinary.

I'm wondering today how you feel about Jesus as *your* Redeemer.

> **In as few or as many words as you would like, describe your relationship with Jesus.**

If you don't know Jesus as your personal Savior, I invite you to trust Him now. He can redeem every piece of your story. You can pray this simple prayer and know it will be received in the heavenlies with rejoicing. Or you can adapt it as a reaffirmation of your commitment to follow Him:

Jesus, I know I am a sinner in need of Your salvation. I know You are the Son of God, who came down to earth to live as a human. I know you willingly sacrificed Yourself on the cross so I might have abundant life now and forever. I know You rose from the dead and ascended into heaven. And I know You will return one day to reign over God's holy kingdom. Until that day, fasten my heart to yours. Teach me to walk in union with You so I may know You and love You more and trust You with every piece of my story. I pray these things in Your holy and precious name. Amen.

You have a guardian-redeemer who promises to renew your story. Every broken thing you carry is in the capable hands of a Savior who is beating the darkness.

If you do know Jesus as your personal Savior, I invite you to release your story to Him. You have a guardian-redeemer who promises to renew your story. Every broken thing you carry is in the capable hands of a Savior who is beating the darkness. Every piece of your impossible story has hope in the name of Jesus. Will you trust Him today with it?

Closing Prayer

Jesus, thank You for being my guardian-redeemer. Thank You for the hope and promise of redemption through Your life and sacrifice. Help me to trust You with my story. I believe You can redeem it. I believe You can renew it. I believe You can bring me hope even though what I face today seems hopeless. I believe in You. I believe You. Amen.

Use the space below to add any extra insights and prayers of your own.

Today's Takeaway

Jesus has the power to redeem both our souls and our stories if we surrender them to Him.

The Movement You Can't See

(Ruth 2)

Welcome/Prayer/Icebreaker (5–10 minutes)

Welcome to Session 2 of *Renewed*! This week, we have explored the events surrounding Naomi's return home to Bethlehem. Many instances point to the work of God behind the scenes in *her* story, which helps us to recognize His work in the details of *our* story. Our time as a group will allow space to dive deeper into questions that arose as you worked through the lessons on your own. Today, we will consider the movement of God, the kindness of God, and Jesus as our guardian-redeemer. Begin by opening up in prayer, and then take a few moments to share an act of kindness you either witnessed or took part in this week.

Video (about 20 minutes)

Play the video segment for Week 2. Just below this section you'll find an outline and space to jot down any notes or extra thoughts you may have while watching the video segment.

—Video Notes—

Scriptures: Psalm 34:8; Ruth 2:2-3; Ruth 2:11-13; Ruth 2:19-20; Philippians 4:19;
Psalm 136:1-9; Romans 6:23; Ephesians 1:3-10

God will meet our _____ needs.

God will meet our _____ needs.

God will meet our _____ needs.

Other Insights:

Video Discussion

- Can you recall a time when you felt far away from God's presence? If you feel comfortable, share a few details about that time with the group.
- When you think of your physical needs, what is the first word that comes to mind? What about your emotional needs? And your spiritual needs?
- What are some tangible ways we can encourage one another that God is always moving in our lives, even when we can't feel His presence?

Workbook Discussion

- On Day 1, we learned of God's command for landowners to leave behind some of their harvest so the poor and needy could glean the fields (page 41). How does Acts 4:32-35 reflect the same generous spirit behind the Old Testament law? How might we live out that spirit in our day-to-day lives now?

- What anxieties or worries do you need to turn over to God? (Day 2, page 52)
- What is an example of a tangible way God has shown up in the details of your life?
- On Day 2, we looked at four verses detailing the kindness of God (page 50). Which verse(s) resonated the most with you? Why?
- On Day 2 (pages 50–51), you read several verses related to hiding in God's wings. Which Scripture resonated with you most? Why?
- On Day 3, we discussed how God's unchanging character provided for Naomi's needs and how He answered her prayer by showing kindness to Ruth (pages 54–56). How has God surprised you with providing for your needs abundantly?
- In what ways does Boaz's character resemble the character of Jesus?
- How has the concept of a guardian-redeemer (Day 3, pages 59–60) given you greater insight into Jesus's mission and work?
- What are some ways you can tangibly share the kindness of God with others this week?

Finding Hope (10–15 minutes)

Divide into groups of two or three and discuss the following:

- As you feel comfortable, describe your relationship with Jesus. (Refer to your comments on Day 3, page 59.) How long have you known Him? If you trust Him as your personal Savior, what prompted you to dedicate your life to Him?
- What part(s) of your story are you trusting Jesus to redeem (Day 1, page 44)?
- In what areas do you need God to provide for you abundantly (Day 3, page 55)?

Closing Prayer (5 minutes)

End your group time together by sharing any prayer requests within the group. You may nominate one person to pray for all requests or you may feel comfortable as a group having all members pray together. Ask God to remind you that as your guardian-redeemer, Jesus has the power to redeem your story.

Week 3

The Intersection of Our Action and God's Plan

(Ruth 3)

He is before all things,
and in him all things hold together.
(Colossians 1:17)

I tried to focus as my doctor explained the ramifications of the diagnosis I had just been given. I was a fitness instructor. I ate well and took care of my body. I made a living teaching other people how to be healthy. Now I was being told that my body was, quite literally, falling apart.

None of it made sense. In an hour's time, all I had known about my world had unraveled. I was left with a deep awareness that the control I once thought I had over my life was a myth. My feelings were not unlike what a friend had expressed to me when her husband lost his job, or when another friend had to leave all she had known in her hometown of thirty years to move across the state, or the grief I had processed as a child when my mother died. When life starts to spin out of control around us, it's easy to wonder if God is in control.

Later, I sat in the carpool line waiting to pick my son up from school. He jumped in the car with a pile of library books about the creation of the earth. We sat around the table that night reading through information on the sun and each of the planets, the various ecosystems around our world, and the diverse multitude of plant and animal species covering the earth. I was struck with the thought that the God who set the universe in motion is the same God who holds my life in His hands. Surely, a God who created the entire universe with such artistic intelligence and beauty would not be uninvolved in the details of my life.

When the world as we know it feels like it's falling apart, we can rejoice in the knowledge that there is One who is never caught off guard and works all things for our good. From the most intricate of details to the broadest of plans, Jesus is behind them all. We can take a deep breath knowing Jesus feels its exhale. We can rise in the morning to face our day with confidence because we know Jesus holds every piece of it in His hands. We can face the unknown courageously because He is already there. We can place our life in His hands with peace, because He holds all of it together.

Naomi felt like her life was falling apart, but she was not willing to give up. Perhaps that's because she knew her life was in good hands, God's hands.

Day 1: Hopeful, Not Helpless

Just do something, I whispered to myself. Anything. It doesn't matter what it is, just do something. I should have been getting out of bed that morning, but instead I sat on the edge, paralyzed.

Scripture Focus

Ruth 3:1-7

We don't have to figure out the next week, the next year, or even the next few days, but we can take baby steps.

I felt both hopeless and helpless. Hard stories can do that to us all. I knew God was ultimately in control, but when it came to the small decisions I still had to make in each day, I was frozen. The realization that I was living with a story I could not change trickled down to the everyday choices I faced. I couldn't decide what clothes to wear or what to eat for breakfast. Should I go the park for a walk or maybe just the neighborhood streets? Did any of it matter or was I expected to just blindly move through the numbing reality?

God whispered an answer that pulled me out of my crippled state of mind: *baby steps.*

We can take baby steps. We don't have to figure out the next week, the next year, or even the next few days, but we can take baby steps.

Those baby steps give us the courage to take action on the pieces of our story we can change as we wait for God to move expectantly on the things we *can't.*

Like Naomi in today's passage, I put two feet on the floor and stood up. You can too.

Read Ruth 3:1-7, and answer the questions below.

Where are the characters in the beginning of this passage?

Briefly describe what Naomi tells Ruth to do.

Where are the characters at the end of this passage?

Setting the Scene

Much of the action in today's reading takes place on a threshing floor, which was used to harvest the grain pulled from the fields. The farmer would pile the un-threshed stalks of grain in the center of the floor, and perhaps would then have donkeys pull a sledge around the grain in a circle. A threshing sledge was like a big sled with teethlike rocks on the bottom, used to separate grain that *can* be used from the grain that *cannot.* The donkey would pull the sledge around the circle until all the good grain had been culled out from the unusable grain. The unusable grain was called chaff, and it included things like husks, pods, and shells.[1]

In verse 2, Naomi mentions that Boaz would be

_____ **barley on the threshing floor.**

To fully separate the chaff from the good grain, the farmer would toss the threshed grain into the air and the wind would blow the chaff away as the good grain fell back down to the earth. This is called winnowing.[2]

The farmer, in this case Boaz, would often spend the night on the threshing floor to protect the grain.[3] Remember this is still in the days when the judges ruled and people did whatever they wanted. One couldn't be too careful.

Extra Insight

You can read other examples about the threshing floor in Deuteronomy 25:4; Isaiah 28:28; Isaiah 41:15-16; and Micah 4:13.

Motivated by the desire to find Ruth a proper and lasting home, Naomi considers the knowledge that Boaz is their guardian-redeemer. And then, rising from the ashes of her earlier defeat, she takes action.

The Deeper Story
What does Ruth 3:1-7 tell us about the human characters in this particular narrative?
Does this passage tell us something about God? If so, what does it say?
Does this passage give us hints that God is at work? If so, what are they?

Steps of Faith

I have to be honest with you. This is probably my most favorite moment of Naomi's story. That's likely because I know firsthand the crippling effects of living with a story you don't like and can't change. The result? You feel like you have no control and it becomes difficult to move forward, even with the smallest of decisions.

Can you recall a moment when your story made you feel paralyzed?

How did you respond?

Were you able to resolve the feeling that you had no control? Explain.

In today's reading, Naomi begins to parse out what is known and unknown at this point in her story. She knows:

- God is answering her prayers.
- The harvest season has been abundant for her and Ruth.
- There is a man who has shown incredible kindness to Ruth.
- The man is a family member and guardian-redeemer for Naomi and Ruth.
- The harvest season is over and it is time to winnow the barley on the threshing floor.
- Her guardian-redeemer will be on the threshing floor.

There is an opportunity on the horizon. What Naomi doesn't know is what happens next. But her courage is building, and she has an idea.

What prompts Naomi's initiative to send Ruth to the threshing floor (v. 1)?

How does the desire to find Ruth a proper home and husband echo Naomi's early desires for Ruth and Orpah in Ruth 1:8-9?

What might this tell you about Naomi and Ruth's relationship?

Naomi and Ruth are dear to one another. This much is clear in their actions. Ruth has been virtuous and resourceful to supply food for both Naomi and herself. But Naomi is concerned for her daughter-in-law and longs for her to find true rest in the home of someone who can take care of her.

In chapter 3, what does Naomi tell Ruth to do in verse 3?

Let's clear up the elephant in the room that may be tromping through your head right now. Was Naomi telling Ruth to get dolled up for Boaz? No. Rather, Naomi's instructions likely implied that Ruth should change out of her mourning cloths into normal clothing.[4] Another possibility is that Ruth's "best clothes" were merely a "large outer garment" to protect her identity until the opportune moment when Boaz was finished eating and drinking.[5] Either way, we can remove any fanciful notions about Ruth donning the equivalent of a little black dress with the intention of seducing Boaz.

But she does go to the threshing floor with the intention of making it known she is available for marriage. Christopher Ash says of this passage, "There is no sexual immorality in this scene, but there are strong hints of intimacy to come."[6]

Glance back at our discussion from Week 1, Day 2 (page 23) on God's law for levirate marriage. Jot down any notes here to jog your memory about its details.

What about the context for levirate marriage might suggest that Naomi's plan of action is a leap of faith and not merely the hope for an arranged marriage?

Here is something else Naomi knows about her situation: the levirate marriage was a law provided *by God* to care for widows such as herself and Ruth. Boaz was a man *of God* who had shown considerable kindness to Ruth and Naomi. Rather than throw up her hands because her story seemed impossible, Naomi chooses to take action on the parts of it she *could* change because she had faith that God would move in the parts she *couldn't*.

What parts of your story are completely out of your control?

What are some parts of your story you can change?

> **God doesn't call plays out of a playbook from the clouds in the sky. He wants to walk with us along every step of our story, holding our hand when we are unsure of the plan.**
>
> *Your word is a lamp for my feet,*
> *a light on my path.*
>
> (Psalm 119:105)

God has ultimate control of our stories and graciously invites us to cowrite them with Him, but He doesn't show us the whole road map. He leads us one step at a time. This can feel like He is trying to withhold important pieces of our future from us, but perhaps the truth is that He would rather partner with us every step of the way.

God is a relational God. He wants to be in relationship with us. That's part of the reason we study His Word, so we can connect with Him on a more intimate level. God doesn't call plays out of a playbook from the clouds in the sky. He wants to walk with us along every step of our story, holding our hand when we are unsure of the plan. He wants us to develop the ability to trust Him with our stories no matter what they look like. And the best way to do that is one step at a time.

If we commit to knowing His Word and spending time with Him so that we know His heart and learn to hear His voice, God will guide us as we discern our next step (Psalm 119:105). We don't have to feel paralyzed. *When our stories leave us feeling helpless, we can find hope by walking in step with God.*

Baby Steps

If what lies ahead in your story feels overwhelming, take a step back and consider what is right in front of you. You don't have to know the whole story. God knows that and you can trust that He is working for your good. But taking action on even a small task can equip you with the confidence and assurance for the next step. It's okay to take baby steps.

When we were newlyweds, my husband came home from work one day to find me vigorously cleaning the baseboards. We were expecting company and the process of cleaning our entire house overwhelmed me. So, I cleaned the baseboards instead.

I didn't know how to articulate it then, but the issue wasn't that our baseboards were all that dirty. It was that big tasks sent me into paralysis mode. I've learned over the years to break things into chunks, or at least make my mind think that's what I'm doing. I did it earlier tonight cleaning the kitchen after dinner.

- Things needed to be cleaned on every counter. (Overwhelming!)
- Hey, just start with the spoons. (Okay, I can do that.)
- Baby step from the spoons to the plates to the pots. (Hey, this isn't so bad.)
- Voila, my kitchen is clean again. (Yippee!)

Big things turned into small tasks are easier to swallow.

What big things do you have on your plate today?

What is one small thing you can do to get you to the next step?

Sometimes walking with a hard story means walking in baby steps. If it feels too big, just start with what you can get done in five minutes. You'll feel better checking something off the list and if you're like me, the momentum from that first baby step—along with God's grace and guidance—will carry you to the finish line.

I think Naomi knew this when she put her plan in motion. She trusted what God could do and then she moved forward with the tasks she could take part in.

You are not helpless. You are not without guts or grit. You also are not alone. Keep putting one foot in front of the other until God lights the next part of your path. He is walking with you every step of the way.

Closing Prayer

Father, thank You for walking with me in my story. I want to stay connected with You as I take the next step. Give me the courage to know how to move forward and the peace to trust You with everything else. Reveal to me my best next steps and protect my mind from being overwhelmed. I am thankful You are here with me. Amen.

Today's Takeaway

When our stories leave us feeling helpless, we can find hope by walking in step with God.

Use the space below to add any extra insights and prayers of your own.

Day 2: A Partnership of Supernatural Proportions

Scripture Focus

Ruth 3:8-15

I hate cooking chicken. To be straightforward, unless we are talking about homemade bread or cheesy grits, talent in the kitchen is not one of my gifts. Handling the insides of America's favorite dinner bird could quite possibly be one of my enemies. Animal proteins, in general, are just too complicated for my limited culinary skills. Which is why one of my favorite times of the day is when my husband comes home from work.

If we happen to be having chicken for dinner, I confess that I strategically time our meal so Tom can help me prepare it. I get everything else ready and let him handle the chicken. It's not just that I am a lousy poultry chef; I enjoy cooking dinner with my husband. We work well together, and between our combined skills, we can get dinner on the table faster than if he or I were working alone. It also usually turns out to be a more satisfying meal. Our skills complement each other to produce a more pleasant dining experience for our family.

In our household, teamwork does indeed make the dinner dream work. This is true of most things in life, but perhaps that's because God promotes the idea of partnership in getting things done.

Read Ruth 3:8-15, and answer the questions below.

What does Ruth ask Boaz to do with his garment?

How does Boaz respond?

What new character in the story does Boaz mention?

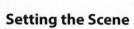

Setting the Scene

Today we continue the scene at the threshing floor. Ruth has done as Naomi instructed and approached Boaz at night after he had finished eating and drinking. We got a good visual picture of the scene before us in yesterday's lesson. Now let's get a good understanding of the traditional activities surrounding the threshing process.

There are many reasons why the location of this encounter is significant, but for our purposes we will focus on just one. The threshing floor is synonymous with joy. One commentator notes that in "ancient agricultural practice, winnowing was the festive, joyous climax of the harvest process."[7] When we glance back at Ruth 3:7, we are reminded that Boaz was in good spirits when Ruth approached him. This may have been because the threshing process often included celebratory festivities.[8] We can imagine a feast with hearty laughter and full bellies. This was a joyful process. It was a time to acknowledge God's promise to provide and care for His people and to thank Him for His faithfulness in doing so.

> **Read Isaiah 41:15-16, which offers context on the threshing process. What emotion is expressed at the end of verse 16?**

The harvest season is a season of blessing. The physical setting for this scene is setting our hearts up for the anticipation of something wonderful to come. In Naomi's story and in yours, there is reason to celebrate.

The Deeper Story
What does Ruth 3:8-15 tell us about the human characters in this particular narrative?
Does this passage tell us something about God? If so, what does it say?

> **Does this passage give us hints that God is at work? If so, what are they?**

God's Storytellers

For our purposes in studying this passage, let's try to resist the urge to romanticize the connection between Ruth and Boaz. What's more, many commentators agree, as expressed by Nancy M. Tischler, that "'if this is a love story, it is primarily the love between Ruth and Naomi,' not Ruth and Boaz."[9]

As I've mentioned earlier in this study, I am a self-professed Disney nerd. Given the above statement, I cannot help but think of the year the Disney movie *Frozen* was released. Moviegoers were collectively surprised when the major plotline of the movie revealed a familial love story between two sisters and not a romantic love story between man and woman. It's with this frame of mind I want us to continue reading. Although we learned yesterday that the goal behind Naomi's plan was to secure a husband for Ruth, Ruth's actions are rooted in her love for Naomi. Ruth and Naomi are fiercely dedicated to one another.

> **Is there someone in your life who you feel as strong a connection with as the one displayed between Ruth and Naomi? If so, briefly describe your relationship:**

Returning to our passage, Boaz awakes in the middle of the night to find Ruth lying near him. Remember from yesterday's lesson that her "best clothes" might have served to conceal her identity, which may be why Boaz questions her identity. Ruth is bold in her response.

> **According to Ruth, what gives Boaz the right to spread the corner of his garment over her (v. 9)?**

Ruth tells Boaz that he is a guardian-redeemer to Ruth and Naomi. But her request that he spread his garment over her is clear and bold. She is asking Boaz to marry her![10]

If you are a visual learner like me, refer to Deuteronomy 22:12 (in the margin) and then draw a simple sketch of what Boaz's garment cloak might have looked like.

Make tassels on the four corners of the cloak you wear.

(Deuteronomy 22:12)

You'll remember from our lesson from Week 2, Day 2 on the study of Ruth 2:12 (page 50), that Boaz tells Ruth she has taken refuge under the wings of the God of Israel. That verse is a beautiful one to meditate on, but there's also a beautiful connection to his comments then and our reading today. When Ruth asks Boaz to cover her with his garment, there's an idiom at play. Commentator Christopher Ash notes that "the word 'wing' literally means the corner of a garment."[11] We can find an example of the same idiom in Ezekiel, where the Lord uses it to describe his love for Israel:

> *"Later I passed by, and when I looked at you and saw that you were old enough for love, I spread the corner of my garment over you and covered your naked body. I gave you my solemn oath and entered into a covenant with you, declares the Sovereign LORD, and you became mine."*
>
> **(Ezekiel 16:8)**

Read Ezekiel 16:8 above and circle any words or thoughts that are similar or relevant to what we are studying in Ruth.

Now think about these words of God being spoken directly to you. What feelings arise when you read them in this way?

Through Jesus, God's covenant promise of love extends to both you and me. God's love surrounds us. Our stories may feel broken, and we are not always protected from trouble. Yet God's sovereignty and ultimate protection are certain. We are His, now and forever. And there is nothing that can ever separate us from His love—nothing that might happen to us, and nothing that we might do. Our stories are His. When we wake in the morning and mourn the path we must take, God covers us with His garment. When we hurt because our story is too much to bear, His cloak of comfort is warm and soothing. When we are unsure of what lies ahead, God tucks His covering of assurance in a little tighter. We are forever safe in the refuge of His wings.

Take a moment to think of all the things in your story that still bring anxiety, fear, or grief. Write each one underneath the wings below. As you do, you might even repeat out loud the words of Ezekiel 16:8, reminding yourself that God's love covers every single piece of your story.

The words of Ezekiel 16:8 are beautiful and precious to any child of God. They were evidence of God's love delivered to His people by His human spokesperson, Ezekiel. Combined with today's passage from Ruth, they also point us to a human partnership with God of supernatural proportions.

One of my favorite things about studying the Bible is the overall story it tells of God's partnership with humanity. God is the sovereign Creator of the universe, speaking it into existence with His voice alone. He doesn't *need* us to enact His plan or accomplish His purpose. And yet, He chooses to partner with us anyway. The Bible tells the story of God's partnership with humanity to bring about His desired will. We are His storytellers. Directed by His Word, prompted by the Holy Spirit, and executed by our own free will, we deliver the story of God's love to the world around us.

Consider the events from our reading today. Even though Naomi isn't present in today's passage, let's think about what is happening from her perspective.

How might the events in today's reading affect Naomi?

How might her story change as a result of Ruth's actions?

Ruth and Boaz are God's storytellers, delivering His plan for Naomi through their actions. Naomi doesn't know it yet, but God is partnering with the human characters of this story to bring her hope. The same is true for you and me. *The hope of God is often delivered through human hands.*

Faster Together

Because we live and breathe and move within the constructs of a fallen world, there will be parts of our story we simply cannot change. For what is unchangeable, we can trust that God will bring the right people into our lives to bring us hope and carry out His will.

Is there someone in your life in the past week or month who has brought you the hope of God? Explain.

How was it delivered and what impact did it have on you?

Who in your life has made the largest impact on your faith thus far?

We can always rely on God to deliver hope to us in His perfect way. But let's flip that around a bit. If we are still living and breathing and moving on this earth, we also have a responsibility to bring hope to the world around us. You are not

the only one walking around with a hard story. I do not say this in any way to downplay your situation or shame you, but rather to spur you into action.

One of the greatest lies we can tell ourselves is that we are alone in our suffering. The stories may look different, but the world suffers alongside us.

Consider those within your respective groups below. Spend a few moments in prayer asking God to reveal individuals in those groups who need the hope of God. And then ask Him to guide your steps in taking action to deliver it. Write down the ideas God gives you.

How could I bring the hope of God to:

Someone in my family

Someone in my friend group

Someone in my church

Someone in my workplace

Someone in my neighborhood

The actions you take today on behalf of God can change the course of someone else's story.

Someone in my town

You are God's storyteller. The actions you take today on behalf of God can change the course of someone else's story. Lift your chin and open your eyes.

Everyone struggles with challenges in this broken world, but one challenge does not trump another.

How can we love those around us when we are hurting too?

First, we can remember that the decision to open our heart to others doesn't diminish the comfort we'll receive from God. God's power to soothe isn't limited. He is capable of healing your heart even as He comforts another. Perhaps a broken story is one that God can use the mightiest to comfort others. There may be painful moments as we expose our vulnerabilities, but He will tenderly walk us through each one with grace.

I remember the moment I found out our second pregnancy would result in a miscarriage. My husband and I were devastated. But more than that, I was ashamed. Even though it wasn't true, I felt like I had done something to cause it. Not wanting to share the news with anyone, I resigned for months to grieve alone. God was tender with me in that place of solace, but it wasn't until I shared my story with a friend who had also suffered a miscarriage that the real healing began. I opened my heart to encourage her, but God used our honest conversations and prayers to release me from the guilt and shame I felt over losing a child. God allowed our collective experience to bring us peace.

Second, we can release our loved ones from the standard we hold ourselves to. Not everyone will move through hard stories in the same way that we do. Our family and friends are our neighbors. One of the ways we can love them best is to acknowledge that their journeys are just as valid as ours, no matter how different.

Both my husband and I have walked through the loss of our fathers. Our responses to that grief were very different, but each of them was necessary in our individual ways of processing bereavement. I tend to withdraw inward wanting stillness and space, while my husband seeks physical activity and connection with others. Neither of these responses is right or wrong; they both are simply manifestations of a creative God making each one of us uniquely different. Tom and I don't always succeed at this, but we try to give each other freedom to grieve in ways that look different from our own, without judgment.

God desires for each of us to grow wiser and closer to Him, but we'll do it faster if we do it together. Open hearts and open minds help us deliver God's hope.

Closing Prayer

Father, thank You for covering me with Your love in every moment. Thank You for putting people in my life to bring hope. Thank You for choosing to partner with me to bring Your love into the world. Give me eyes to see those who are hurting. Give me wisdom to know how to love them well. Give me courage to act and deliver Your hope to my family, friends, and community. Amen.

Today's Takeaway

The hope of God is often delivered through human hands.

Use the space below to add any extra insights and prayers of your own.

Day 3: The Cliffhanger

Scripture Focus

Ruth 3:16-18

I'm wondering today if you have ever played the game Mouse Trap? It's a children's game, usually played with two to four players. Players work to build an elaborate mouse-trapping set, which works sort of like a domino game put in motion by the drop of a small metal ball onto the set. Each player selects a mouse for their playing piece and the object of the game is to not let your mouse get caught in the trap.

The mouse-trapping set follows the same course: you drop the ball at the start of the course, which triggers a motion on the next stage of the course, which triggers another motion, and so on and so on, until the cage is dropped and the mouse is caught. The only variation is at the end to see which player's mouse will get caught.

Today's reading reminds me a little bit of Mouse Trap. The stage is set. The pieces are in place. The only variable option is how will it end. There are two guardian-redeemers on the stage now. Which one will complete the story?

Brace yourselves for a cliff-hanger because we might have to wait to find out.

Read Ruth 3:16-18, and answer the questions below.

What did Boaz give to Ruth to take home?

Who was this gift for?

In verse 18, what unsettled matter does Naomi refer to?

Setting the Scene

After the dramatic events of yesterday, two characters head home from the threshing floor. One other character is likely wide awake and restless wondering how it all turned out. Indeed, Naomi's first question to Ruth is, "How did it go, my daughter?"

> **Translate Naomi's question to Ruth in verse 16 in your own words. What information do you think she really wanted to know?**

Recall from yesterday's reading that Boaz agreed to marry Ruth. But he revealed to her that there was another guardian-redeemer who was closer in kin to Naomi than he. This is wonderful news for Naomi! Someone is willing to purchase Elimelek's property and look out for his family. Actually, there may be two who are willing. Redemption for Naomi and Ruth is in play, but the question looms...who will it be?

The Deeper Story
What does Ruth 3:16-18 tell us about the human characters in this particular narrative?
Does this passage tell us something about God? If so, what does it say?
Does this passage give us hints that God is at work? If so, what are they?

Stay Calm

We like quick answers and easy answers, don't we? I vividly remember the bookshelf in the back corner of the living room in my childhood home. It was one of my favorite spots in the house because on the bottom of that bookshelf was a twenty-two-volume encyclopedia set. When I had a question about anything in the world, this was the spot I would go to first. If that didn't resolve my curiosity, I would plan a trip to the local library. It often took time to find the answer, but I didn't mind. I enjoyed the process of discovery.

Today, if I have a question about something, I'll just do a quick Google search on my phone or the internet and I'll have thousands of results in less than a second. Modern technology has trained us to expect instant answers.

We often want God to answer our prayers right away, and we have little interest in the process of discovery while we wait.

The same expectation might be said of our prayers. We often want God to answer our prayers right away, and we have little interest in the process of discovery while we wait.

If you could snap your fingers and get an instant answer, what prayer request would you like God to answer immediately?

In response to Naomi's question about the previous night, we are simply told that Ruth relayed the facts of what Boaz had done. Then she delivers a gift from Boaz: six measures of barley grain. The way the author of Ruth shapes this part of the story directs our attention away from Naomi's question and redirects it toward Naomi's gift from Boaz.

Why might the author want us to focus on Boaz's gift to Naomi?

Fill in the blank from Boaz's words in verse 17 below.

"Don't go back to your mother-in-law

_____."

We've seen these words before, but they were spoken by Naomi.

Turn back to Ruth 1:21 and fill in the blank from Naomi's words there.

"I went away full, but the Lᴏʀᴅ has brought me back

_____."

The words you just used to fill in the blank from both verses are the exact same Hebrew word *reqam*.[13] But they are used to imply two different things. Once more, the concept of contrast appears in Naomi's story. She began the journey to Bethlehem empty, but Boaz does not want Ruth to return to Naomi empty-handed.

What has changed for Naomi between Ruth 1:21 and Ruth 3:17?

Who is responsible for the changes in her story?

Why might Boaz be concerned about Ruth going back to Naomi empty-handed?

It is likely that Boaz sent Ruth home with the gift of barley for Naomi to clearly announce his intentions to marry Ruth as long as the other guardian-redeemer does not interfere.[14] It would be the ancient Israelite equivalent of a suitor purchasing an engagement ring and meeting with his love's father before proposing to her. But as the reader, we have the gift of hindsight in this story. We know Boaz's desire to send Ruth home with a full cloak of grain answers an unspoken prayer for Naomi: she was empty before, but she will not be empty-handed now. Famine is no longer a threat. Provision for her and her daughter-in-law will soon not be a dilemma.

For those of us processing the full scope of Naomi's story, Boaz's gift symbolizes not just his intention, but also *hope*. Hope is on the way for Naomi. It's dripping off the pages of the Bible so sweetly we can taste it. As we ponder this thrilling reality for Naomi, my question to you today is related. What keeps you from giving up? What gives you hope?

What gives you hope?

We have one more chapter left in Naomi's story, but today's passage records her final spoken words. She knows that something good is coming tomorrow, but she doesn't quite know how it will all turn out.

Read Ruth 3:18 below and circle Naomi's first word to Ruth.

Then Naomi said, "Wait, my daughter, until you find out what happens. For the man will not rest until the matter is settled today."

(Ruth 3:18)

Wait. This is one of Naomi's last recorded words in her story. Conversationally in Hebrew, Naomi may as well have said "sit tight" or even "stay calm."[15] This from the woman who changed her name to *call-me-bitter* in the beginning of this story. It would appear that Naomi has undergone quite a transformation, has she not?

Imagine Naomi sitting at the table with you and me today. The three of us are sharing a cup of coffee and talking about our stories. As you are sharing about yours, Naomi lowers her coffee cup and turns to look you tenderly in the eyes and says, "Sit tight, sister...stay calm."

What in your story would Naomi be referring to?

It is my prayer for you that Naomi's last words would stay with you, deeply planted in your heart until the moment you can turn to the Lord and say, I *was empty but now* I *am full.* The reason I know that you can do this is because of the last words of the bigger story from which we are reading.

Turn to the last book of the Bible and read Revelation 22:20-21.
Write down the two verses word for word.

Naomi's story at this point is a cliff-hanger, but ours is not. Jesus is coming soon. A certain promise of hope looms on the horizon. When Jesus returns, the physical pain you carry will be healed. The emotional sorrow you know all too well will be erased from memory. And the mental fear you navigate about the future will be replaced with unceasing joy. And until He returns, His grace will keep us steady through all those things. Even so, come Lord Jesus.

Psalm 27:14 has long been a favorite of mine: "*Wait for the* L<small>ORD</small>; / *be strong and take heart / and wait for the* L<small>ORD</small>." Until we wait for Jesus to return, for our stories to change and for our hearts to turn from empty to full, this is a good verse to meditate on.

As you consider Psalm 27:14, what would help you put this psalm into practice?

Wait and Hope

A few years ago, I opened my email inbox to see a message from a dear friend. We knew each other from fitness classes, but she was a photographer and had sent me a digital copy of a photo she had recently taken. She said she knew I would like it because it felt very symbolic for me. She was right. In the foreground of the photo you could see latticework from what looked like an iron fence or gate of some sort. As your gaze continued to look through and beyond the fence, the background revealed a stone memorial covered in moss and lichen. Framed just perfectly among the moss were three simple words: *wait and hope.*

I had a visceral response to the photo. It moved me so deeply but I didn't know why at the time. Now I do. It professed the essence of a believer's heart clinging to Jesus in a broken world. *We wait on the Savior to return while we place our hope in Him to renew our story.*

Is it easy or difficult to believe that Jesus can renew your story? Explain.

²³Not only so, but we ourselves, who have the firstfruits of the Spirit, groan inwardly as we wait eagerly for our adoption to sonship, the redemption of our bodies. ²⁴For in this hope we were saved. But hope that is seen is no hope at all. Who hopes for what they already have? ²⁵But if we hope for what we do not yet have, we wait for it patiently.

(Romans 8:23-25)

Today's Takeaway

We wait on the Savior to return while we place our hope in Him to renew our story.

One of our goals throughout this study is to consistently seek the unchanging character of God as revealed in the Book of Ruth. In the Book of Romans, Paul writes of an unchanging promise that many believers readily cling to—and one you can trust for yourself too.

> *And we know that in all things God works for the good of those who love him, who have been called according to his purpose.*
>
> (Romans 8:28)

That verse may be familiar to you, but if you read a few verses prior to it, you'll discover the secret to believing that promise.

Read the promise of Romans 8:23-25 in the margin. Circle every time the word *wait* appears and underline every appearance of the word *hope*.

Wait and hope. This is the secret to living with a story we don't like. In the meantime, we will trust that God is working for our good, in the same way that He has worked in Naomi's story.

Her story isn't over just yet, and neither is yours. There is still space to dream.

Closing Prayer

Father, thank You for the hope of Christ. I trust that He is coming soon and that He will keep me steady until that day. When I close my eyes tonight, I will put my hope in You. And tomorrow when I wake, I will wait expectantly for You to move in my details. Give me the peace to stay calm and the courage to cling to You when I am impatient. I trust You with my story. Amen.

Use the space below to add any extra insights and prayers of your own.

The Intersection of Our Action and God's Plan

(Ruth 3)

Welcome/Prayer/Icebreaker (5–10 minutes)

Welcome to Session 3 of *Renewed*! This week, we considered the results of God's partnership with us to accomplish His will as we watched Naomi move from helpless to hopeful. Naomi found the courage to take bold steps in her story and her last words reminded us to stay calm as we yearn for Christ's return. Our time as a group will allow space to dive deeper into questions that arose as you worked through the lessons on your own. Today we will consider the baby steps of faith you can take to avoid feeling helpless, our role as God's storytellers, and the tension we hold as we wait for and hope in Jesus. Begin by opening up in prayer, and then take a few moments to share your favorite comfort food to indulge in when life is stressful.

Video (about 20 minutes)

Play the video segment for Week 3. Just below this section you'll find an outline and space to jot down any notes or extra thoughts you may have while watching the video segment.

—Video Notes—

Scriptures: 2 Corinthians 9:8; Ruth 3:1; Ruth 3:18; Hebrews 11:1

A confident faith moves forward even when the _____ is unknown.

A confident faith is comfortable in _____ for God to move.

A confident faith points to the glory of God's _____ and _____, instead of our own.

Other Insights:

Video Discussion

- Describe one or two things happening in your life right now that you cannot control. Is there something you can act on anyway, despite the reality of your situation? If so, share it with your group.
- What is the most difficult thing about waiting on God?
- What are some tangible ways you can place your trust in God today?

Workbook Discussion

- What favorite verse(s) do you turn to when things feel like they are falling apart?

- On Day 1 (page 68), we considered the tendency to feel overwhelmed to the point of indecision when we feel like we have no control over our story. Can you share a moment when your story made you feel paralyzed?
- What are some baby steps you take to help you get through a difficult day (Day 1, page 71)?
- On Day 2 (page 76–77), we discussed our responsibility as God's storytellers to deliver His love into the world. How does 1 John 3:17-18 bring more insight into this calling?
- Day 2 talked about God using people to bring you hope (page 77). Who has done that for you in the past?
- "We often want God to answer our prayers right away, and we have little interest in the process of discovery while we wait" (Day 3, page 82). What is God doing in you as you wait through your hard story?
- If you could have one prayer request instantly answered, what would it be (Day 3, page 82)?
- What are you most looking forward to about Christ's return?
- What is one tangible way you can bring hope to your community this week?

Finding Hope (10–15 minutes)

Divide into groups of two or three and discuss the following:

- Do you agree that waiting and hoping are the secret to living with a story we don't like (Day 3, page 85)? Why or why not?
- How do you lean into the truth of Romans 8:23-25 to help you move through the obstacles you may face in your day-to-day life?
- What gives you hope about your story?

Closing Prayer (5 minutes)

End your group time together by sharing any prayer requests within the group. You may nominate one person to pray for all requests or you may feel comfortable as a group having all members pray together. Ask God to give you the courage to be His storyteller to the world as you wait and hope for Christ's return.

Week 4

The God Who Rescues, Redeems, and Renews

(Ruth 4)

When the LORD restored the fortunes of Zion,
we were like those who dreamed.
(Psalm 126:1)

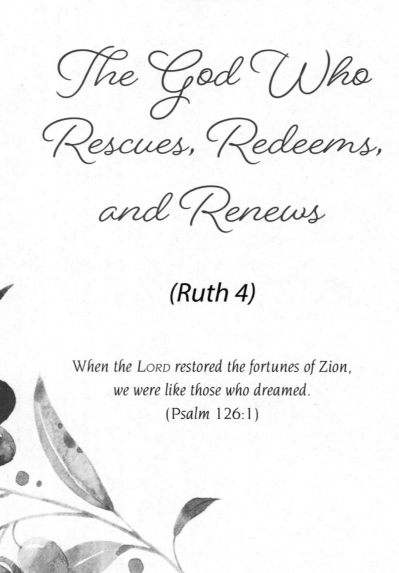

It seemed nearly impossible. I had done it before, of course, but the thought of doing it again brought me to tears. Finding the space to plant new dreams in my heart felt too risky and too dangerous. Surely it would be a prescription for sorrow. I didn't know how to come up with a new dream. It was easier to stop hoping.

The only dream I ever had was to be the mother of a large family. Growing up as an only child, I longed to fill my adult home with the laughter and chaos from as many children as the Lord saw fit to give me, and I had hoped that it would be at least four. Messy handprints on the walls, a dinner table with no room for more chairs, loud voices interrupting one another with news to share, watching brothers and sisters become best friends... I wanted all the craziness and the blessings that came with large families.

After our firstborn, my husband and I were well on our way to building our dream family. But along with a miscarriage in our second pregnancy came the news that biological children were no longer an option. And because of the medical condition I'd been diagnosed with, our future was uncertain, so adoption wasn't an option either.

Bitterness and grief set in as it appeared the only way I was going to fulfill my dream was to watch other mothers live theirs. I grew tired of answering questions from well-meaning friends and family members wanting to know when we were going to have another child.

I remember many quiet mornings spent folding my son's clothes and asking God why He would plant such a dream in my heart only to make me mourn for it. And what I've learned so far is that the greatest capacity to comfort others is born from shared heartbreak. I've developed some of the most encouraging and godly relationships with women who have experienced a similar journey.

But God is teaching me something else, also. Amid the ruins of my broken dream lie the seeds of another. It's a dream that I never would have dared to imagine and it is covered in the handiwork of my heavenly Father. An unfulfilled dream isn't the end of hope; it might just be the beginning of a new work of God in your life. The words of Psalm 126 remind me that the Lord loves to restore broken dreams.

Naomi's story is evidence of this truth as well.

Day 1: Hope for the Future

Scripture Focus

Ruth 4:1-10

We are a goldendoodle family. Our first goldendoodle, Dixie, was the best family dog, and when she passed away in 2014, we knew we would eventually get another one. So, when a friend referred us to a local family that had a litter of goldendoodles last summer, we thought it might be the right time to welcome another doodle into our home.

We visited the new puppies and Thomas handpicked the one that would come home with us in a few weeks. We named her Nala and began gathering our puppy supplies. And then the breeder called.

Nala had a heart murmur.

We knew that it was not uncommon for young puppies to develop an innocent heart murmur that would soon go away, but there was no way to know for sure. We had two choices: we could keep her and take the chance that we might face costly veterinary care for her if it didn't go away, or we could wait for a puppy from the litter planned for the next year.

I talked it over with my husband and his response was this: "We're already in love with her. If she has a health imperfection, that's just how we roll in this family. We'll keep her."

His response spoke of his willingness to take risks on the things that he loves, no matter the cost, but it reminded me of the actions of our Savior. I think today's reading may do the same.

Read Ruth 4:1-10 and answer the questions below.

Whom did Boaz meet with at the town gate?

Why does the other guardian-redeemer decide not to redeem Elimelek's estate?

In verse 10, what additional benefit does Naomi's family receive from Boaz's willingness to redeem Elimelek's estate?

Setting the Scene

Even though thousands of years separate us from the setting of today's passage in Ruth, it won't be hard to imagine the scene before us. As civil courtrooms go, they are rather similar, whether they are set in the thirteenth century or the twenty-first. Instead of a courthouse, the place for legal transactions in the ancient East was the town gate.[1] Instead of an official jury, there were official witnesses.

In verse 2, who are the witnesses comprised from?

A case is presented, a decision is made and formally agreed upon, and the transaction is legalized.

It is in this manner that Boaz meets with the other guardian-redeemer about Elimelek's estate. We are not given the name of the other guardian-redeemer, but that's probably on purpose. Boaz calls him "friend," but the original language for the reference he uses could be translated as Mr. "So-and-So."[2]

What purpose might the author of Ruth have in not giving us the other guardian-redeemer's name?

If you just wrote some variation of the fact that the identity of the other guardian-redeemer might not be important to the lasting legacy of this story, you would be spot-on. Many scholars agree with this biblical commentator who confirms that "by not naming him, the storyteller indicates that he will lack lasting significance."[3]

However, Mr. So-and-So's character does serve a significant purpose in our reading for today. Let's find it together.

The Deeper Story
What does Ruth 4:1-10 tell us about the human characters in this particular narrative?
Does this passage tell us something about God? If so, what does it say?

Extra Insight

"The gate was the place of legal decision-making. Excavations from the 'gate' in some ancient towns show benches on which people could sit. To sit was the position of authority or doing business."[4] You can see Jesus participating in the same tradition as He sits down to teach in the temple in Luke 4:20.

> **Does this passage give us hints that God is at work? If so, what are they?**

A Future Promise

Who will redeem Elimelek's estate? That is the question for today's court case. Redeeming Elimelek's estate would involve taking responsibility for both Naomi and Ruth, in addition to purchasing Naomi's piece of land that originally belonged to Elimelek. What happened to Naomi's land to begin with? It is possible that Elimelek sold it when they left Bethlehem for Moab,[5] or the situation might have resembled the scenario in 2 Kings 8:1-6, where the land of the Shunammite woman, whose son Elisha had healed, is restored (check it out if you have time).

If it surprises you to learn that Naomi has land, something of value, let me ask you this.

> **Would it surprise you to consider that your story still has purpose?**

When we live with the imperfect, it can be hard to imagine that any good could come of it. Sometimes we believe the brokenness in our stories and that's all we see. We've got blinders on to the possibilities that lie ahead because we can't look past the finality of what we've been dealt. A door has been closed and we can't see the window. Maybe we just need someone to help us find it.

> **In Ruth 4, what is Mr. So-and-So's initial response to Boaz's presentation? (v. 4)**

The other guardian-redeemer agrees quickly to redeem Elimelek's estate. But there's a hitch that perhaps he had not thought of.

> **In verse 5, what additional information does Boaz give to Mr. So-and-So about redeeming Elimelek's estate?**

What is his response after learning this new information?

What reason does he give for the change in his response?

Redemption is costly. Consider the expenses Mr. So-and-So would incur by redeeming Elimelek's estate:

- He would have to take care of Naomi.
- He would have to take care of Ruth.
- He would have to take care of any children he had with Ruth.

If those costs were not enough risk to Mr. So-and-So's estate, there is an additional risk he is likely considering. We can find a comparable explanation of it in the Book of Deuteronomy.

Read Deuteronomy 25:5-6. What information in verse 6 gives us insight into Mr. So-and-So's decision-making process?

Why does the first son carry on the name of the deceased man, rather than the name of the man who redeems his estate?

If Mr. So-and-So were to redeem Elimelek's estate, he would have to marry Ruth. Should he and Ruth have any children together, their first son would be deemed Elimelek's son, not Mr. So-and-So's, and would therefore inherit Elimelek's land.[7] Mr. So-and-So would incur substantial costs by redeeming Elimelek's estate, with no promise for future financial gain. You can see the reasoning for Mr. So-and-So's retraction of his original statement, given the new information Boaz gave him.

On the other hand, Boaz looks to incur the same costs if he agrees to redeem. Briefly skim through Ruth 2 and 3 again, looking for details we picked up about Boaz's character, along with any new insights you may find.

Why might Boaz have been willing to redeem Elimelek's property, even knowing the costs he would incur, when Mr. So-and-So was not?

There is no reason to presume that Mr. So-and-So's decision was rooted in anything other than practicalities.[8] He wasn't sinful. He was logically sound. But redemption doesn't make logical sense. It makes heavenly sense.

We know from Ruth 2 and 3 that Boaz is a godly, upright man of standing who is committed to doing the right thing and always observant of the law. He is kind and generous, an abundant provider who is thoughtful toward the vulnerable, and willing to invite the foreigner, Ruth the Moabitess, into his home. He chooses to become the literal redeemer for Naomi and Ruth.

How does Boaz remind you of Jesus here?

In writing about how Boaz foreshadows the coming Christ, Mitchell Chase says this:

If someone invited you to listen to a story about a redeemer from Bethlehem in Judah who fulfilled and exceeded the law with his acts of mercy and abundant provision before entering into covenant with a bride from the nations, that story could be about Boaz or Jesus. Such is the beauty and brilliance of the Word of God.[9]

The beauty and the brilliance, amen! What Boaz does for Naomi and Ruth, Jesus has done for you on the cross.

Read Colossians 1:19-23 slowly and prayerfully. Make a list of the costs Jesus incurred for you and the blessings you receive from His redemption.

JESUS'S COST   **MY BLESSING**

If these blessings were not enough to make us jump for joy, let's keep reading for one final morsel of goodness in today's passage. When Boaz announces in Ruth 4 that he has redeemed Elimelek's estate, he reminds the witnesses that his choice does not just affect his present time.

What lasting legacy does Boaz mention in verse 10?

What implication does this give for Naomi's story?

At the beginning of the Book of Ruth, Naomi could see only the closed door in front of her. With no prospect for present provision and no hope for a future heir, Naomi thought her story was over. But today brings *hope*.

Like Boaz to Naomi, Jesus promises redemption for us. *Because of Jesus's sacrifice on the cross, our stories have hope for the future*. Pause for a moment to breathe that in. And then place two fingers on either side of your throat. Gently feel around until you locate the steady, consistent pulse emanating from under your skin. And then breathe again. You are still here. Your story is not over. If you have a pulse, you have a purpose. And with Jesus, you have a future promise.

Joy Awaits

No matter the cost, Jesus was determined to redeem your story.

How are you prompted to respond to this truth today?

To honor the sacrifice Jesus made for us, let's be willing to trust that He can redeem our hard story. Lift your heart toward heaven today and acknowledge that Jesus thinks you are worth the cost. You are precious, valued, deeply loved, and eternally accepted. Your story may be ripe with the imperfect, but it is in His perfect hands.

I'm still thinking about our Nala's heart murmur as I write this. The easy way out would have been to return her and wait for a perfect puppy. But if we're waiting for things to be perfect, we might miss out on the things that would bring us the most joy today. How many times have I wasted an opportunity for blessing because I was unwilling to deal with imperfection? If having an incurable genetic disorder has taught me anything, it's that we can't afford the luxury of waiting for all the pieces to fit perfectly. Life will move right along and we might miss the sweetest parts of it if we aren't willing to get our hands dirty.

> If we're waiting for things to be perfect, we might miss out on the things that would bring us the most joy today.

Every day, you and I wake up with things that are broken, imperfect, and ugly. If we trust Him, Jesus promises to transform it all. He's not only working on the broken things in our story, He's also working on the broken things in our hearts. Day after day, baby step after baby step, one divine brush stroke after another, He is redeeming and renewing every detail of our story, until the day when we'll stand perfect in His presence.

A few weeks after we took Nala home, her breeder joined us in praying for her heart. Not long after, we took her to the vet, who happily told us there was no evidence of a heart murmur anymore. We were thrilled and so very thankful. And I can attest that to this very day, she brings us much joy.

Take the leap in trusting Jesus to redeem your story. Say the prayers. Step into the broken. Give all your imperfect pieces to Jesus and trust Him to work. He's waiting to bring you joy.

Closing Prayer

Jesus, thank You for redeeming my life on the cross. Thank You for thinking I was worth the cost. Thank You for the promise of future hope. My story is hard and broken, but I trust You to renew it. Give me the presence of mind to wake up every day with gratitude for Your sacrifice on the cross. Let the knowledge of Your redeeming love give me courage to keep moving forward. Amen.

Use the space below to add any extra insights and prayers of your own.

Today's Takeaway

Because of Jesus's sacrifice on the cross, our stories have hope for the future.

Scripture Focus

Ruth 4:11-15

Day 2: Renewed with Hope

My husband and I were three weeks into a daily prayer commitment over middle school options for my son when we realized we had gotten it all wrong. We are fortunate to live in an area with several choices for schooling, and we wanted to make the right one, especially considering the potentially tumultuous middle school years ahead. We felt like this decision warranted a specific prayer strategy, so we started praying separately over this one thing.

Looming decisions can require dedicated prayer, but God often uses our prayer time to teach us something as we wait for Him to answer. It took my son's favorite breakfast to show us what God needed us to learn.

On any given morning, my son will come down the stairs and request that I make him one of two things: Nutella toast or a Nutella waffle. This is always his request and these are the only two options he ever gives me. Sometimes I make exactly that for him, but a lot of times I'll add a glass of milk, a scrambled egg, and some fresh fruit to his order. Why? Because I know his growing body needs more than what Nutella toast can offer. Balanced meals are better than skimpy ones. Full buffets are even better.

Somewhere around week three-and-a-half of our prayer over the middle school decision, I realized we had presented the exact same request to God: "Hey, God! We've done the research for You and here's what we think is in his best interest. Our son needs to go to *this* school or *this* school. There aren't any other options. So, which is it? Nutella toast or a Nutella waffle?"

But what if we're asking the wrong questions? What if God is waiting to give us the buffet...or shrimp and grits (yes, please)...or something else altogether, but we're too afraid of the unknown to ask for it?

We want control and God wants our trust. Like Naomi's story promises today, the buffet may be waiting when we relinquish control and let God write our story.

> **Read Ruth 4:11-15, and answer the questions below.**
>
> **Who blesses the marriage of Ruth and Boaz?**
>
>
> **What did God enable Ruth to do?**
>
>
> **What has God not left Naomi without?**

Setting the Scene

If we were ever prompted to throw the most massive celebratory feast in response to what we are reading in the Bible, today is that day. Picking up in the same setting where we left yesterday's lesson, at the town gate, we find the witnesses rejoicing over the union of Ruth and Boaz. We learn that God gave Boaz and Ruth a son. And we see the good news that has come to Naomi. I weep with tears of joy, knowing how far of a journey she has come.

Briefly skim through Ruth 1 to remind yourself of where her journey started. And then take a moment to compare, or rather, *contrast* the two settings. List three to five words that you would you use to describe each setting.

Ruth 1   Ruth 4
Bitter   Renewed

There is a colossal sense of relief in today's passage. I hope you feel it tangibly in your soul. If you don't, stop right now and go turn your praise music up loud enough that the neighbors can hear it. Fix yourself your favorite snack, meal, or beverage. And let the corners of your mouth turn upwards with joy on Naomi's behalf.

I wholeheartedly believe that if Naomi were sitting here with us today, she would do the same thing for you. Joy is contagious. And it's about time we celebrated in it.

The Deeper Story
What does Ruth 4:11-15 tell us about the human characters in this particular narrative?
Does this passage tell us something about God? If so, what does it say?
Does this passage give us hints that God is at work? If so, what are they?

Renewal for Our Past, Present, and Future

What began in dark will end in the light. An all-encompassing dedication surrounds the beginning of our reading today. If you look closely at the blessing from the witnesses, you'll notice it has three parts.

Look at verses 11-12, and complete each part of the blessing by finishing each statement below. (If you are reading from a translation other than the NIV, the beginning of each statement may differ from what is listed below.)

Blessing 1: May the LORD make...

Blessing 2: May you have standing...

Blessing 3: Through the offspring...

Consider how each blessing is presented. Do you see a pattern, and if so, what is it?

Each blessing represents three time periods: the past, the present, and the future. The blessing referencing Rachel and Leah recalls the past (Genesis 29–35). The blessing referencing Boaz's standing in Ephrathah alludes to the present. And the blessing about Boaz and Ruth's offspring looks to the future. In full contrast to the emptiness that pervades the beginning of this story, the witnesses' blessing embodies the fullness of any human story—their past, present, and future.

Where you completed each blessing above, label each one with the appropriate time frame: past, present, or future.

What truth might God want us to discover in the way this blessing was written in His Word? Write a one-sentence statement summarizing your thoughts:

Extra Insight

The story of Tamar, Judah, and Perez, which echoes similar, but not identical, themes in the story in Ruth, can be found in Genesis 38.

God's goodness is not just for the here and now. God promises to rescue our past, redeem our present, and renew our future. Although some time passes between the blessing of verses 11-12 and what is recorded starting in verse 13, the same truth is proclaimed. We just get to see it tangibly delivered in Naomi's story.

He will renew your life and sustain you in your old age.
(Ruth 4:15a)

Reread Ruth 4:14-15. In what ways does God:

Rescue Naomi's past...

Redeem her present...

Renew her future...

Relishing in this joy for Naomi, look closely at the cover of this book. You'll notice beautiful olive branches depicted on either side. One side is empty, and the other is full. Trace your fingers along the lovely details of the cover and thank God for His promise to rescue, redeem, and renew. Rejoice with Naomi that God has renewed her story, and then turn your attention to yours.

Like Naomi, God's promise for renewal extends to your past, your present, and your future. Are there mistakes from your past for which you have not sought forgiveness? Are you carrying the betrayal of hurts done to you in the past by others? Has tragedy struck and are you trying to pick up the pieces of a broken story and carry on with your present? Does it seem impossible to consider a future with hope?

Spend a few moments thinking through each time frame of your story and write down any areas that are in need of healing and renewal from your heavenly Father.

My past...

My present...

My future…

As you feel led, say this prayer out loud or write one of your own in the space below:

Father, I release each part of my story—my past, present, and future—into Your hands. I trust You to renew every piece of it. Amen.

If I were sitting next to you right now, I would wrap you in a giant hug, give you a high-five, and help you finish celebrating that party you started at the beginning of this lesson. Releasing our stories to God takes great courage, but it also brings great relief and freedom. I am so proud of you and, more importantly, so is your heavenly Father.

The work does not stop here, however. Like Naomi, trusting God to renew our stories means putting one foot in front of the other as we continually remind ourselves of His promises. So, I want to share with you nine of my favorite Scripture selections to pray when I am clinging to God's promise for renewal.

As you go about your day, spend some time meditating on each one. If a particular verse resonates with you more than the others, jot it down on a note card and tape it up in your home. I display these verses in my kitchen, on my bathroom mirror, on my nightstand, in my office, and on the door on the way out of the house. *God promises to renew our past, our present, and our future.* We can cling to His Word to remind us of this truth.

> Releasing our stories to God takes great courage, but it also brings great relief and freedom.

Nine Verses to Pray When Clinging to God's Promise for Renewal

Past

*"You wearied yourself by such going about,
     but you would not say, 'It is hopeless.'*

> You found renewal of your strength,
> and so you did not faint."
>
> (Isaiah 57:10)

> Create in me a pure heart, O God,
> and renew a steadfast spirit within me.
>
> (Psalm 51:10)

> You were taught, with regard to your former way of life, to put off your old self, which is being corrupted by its deceitful desires; to be made new in the attitude of your minds; and to put on the new self, created to be like God in true righteousness and holiness.
>
> (Ephesians 4:22-24)

Present

> But those who hope in the LORD
> will renew their strength.
> They will soar on wings like eagles;
> they will run and not grow weary,
> they will walk and not be faint.
>
> (Isaiah 40:31)

> Therefore, if anyone is in Christ, the new creation has come: The old has gone, the new is here!
>
> (2 Corinthians 5:17)

> Put on your new nature, and be renewed as you learn to know your Creator and become like him.
>
> (Colossians 3:10 NLT)

Future

> Do not conform to the pattern of this world, but be transformed by the renewing of your mind. Then you will be able to test and approve what God's will is—his good, pleasing and perfect will.
>
> (Romans 12:2)

> Therefore we do not lose heart. Though outwardly we are wasting away, yet inwardly we are being renewed day by day.
>
> (2 Corinthians 4:16)

> He who was seated on the throne said, "I am making everything new!" Then he said, "Write this down, for these words are trustworthy and true."
>
> (Revelation 21:5)

Be Renewed, Live Renewed

You can tell the difference between someone who *hears* the promise of God's renewal and someone who *believes in* the promise of God's renewal by the language of their prayers. There's no shame in the discovery process it may take in getting to the point of full-on, brazen belief that God can renew anything. Our faith walk with God is a collective journey. We may be in different stages, but we are all on the same path.

On the line scale below, draw a heart where you find yourself in the process today.

Hearing   **Believing**

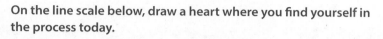

If you placed your heart nearest to the believing end, I rejoice with you! If you placed your heart nearest to the hearing end, I rejoice with you as well! And may I offer a suggestion as we wrap up this day to help move your heart to the freedom side of believing in God's promise to renew your story? *Change the language of your prayers.*

Instead of giving God options for what you think is best for your story, start asking for H*is best* for your life. We may think we have the perfect answers, but only God can orchestrate a story as beautiful and redemptive as Naomi's. Would you trust Him with wild abandon today to orchestrate yours?

As my husband and I were convicted over not trusting God with the answer to our middle school decision, we changed the language of our prayer. Instead of asking for one of two options that we had carefully chosen, we started asking God to simply reveal His best for our family. Period. Because we want the adventure. We want the unknown. We want whatever God has in store for us because only His plan will be in our best interest.

Are you asking God for the buffet or are you settling for Nutella? It will take courage to ask God to rewrite your story, but God is faithful to renew it in His way and in His time.

> **Instead of giving God options for what you think is best for your story, start asking for *His best* for your life.**

Closing Prayer

God, I am changing the language of my prayers today. I relinquish all control of my story to You. I trust You to renew my past, my present, and my future. I don't have to know the outcome of my story because I know You and I cling to Your promises. You are good and gracious and my best interest is in Your plans, not any plans I may have of my own. I am asking You to rewrite my story in a way that only You can. Amen.

Today's Takeaway

God promises to renew our past, our present, and our future.

Use the space below to add any extra insights and prayers of your own.

Day 3: The Promise of Redemption

Scripture Focus

Ruth 4:16-22

At three o'clock in the morning, I woke a five-year-old Thomas up early and bundled us both up in blankets as we walked onto the back porch. We crept up to the screen and quietly waited. In just a few moments, we could see the spiderweb shaking back and forth. Missy was remaking her web, as she was wont to do every night around three o'clock.

Missy was a garden-writing spider, not unlike the spider made famous in *Charlotte's Web*, and she had made her home that particular summer on the other side of our screened-in porch. She was quite menacing to look at as spiders go, but we were so fascinated with her behavior we couldn't stop observing her. Thomas and I watched her all summer.

Over the course of several months, we watched her entire life cycle. We saw her relish in the heat of long summer days, consume a variety of pesky garden bugs, which we were thankful for, and when it was time, we saw her lay her eggs nearby. As the weather turned colder, Missy relocated to another area in our garden. And then she was gone.

We considered ourselves privileged to have watched her entire story play out before us that summer. Missy's story was a part of a much larger story that played out that summer season in our garden.

Not unlike a story that began in a garden some thousands of years ago, yours is part of an even greater one. The most important story ever told.

Read Ruth 4:16-22, and answer the questions below.

Who cared for Ruth and Boaz's child?

What was his name?

Who is Obed's grandson?

Setting the Scene

It is bittersweet to come to the final lesson in our study together. I hope you have relished in the Book of Ruth as much as I have. Ruth is my favorite book of the Bible, and it has been a privilege to walk through it with you, reading it from Naomi's perspective.

As we have considered Naomi's story together, imagine that we did so with a telescope lens fixed on her path. Today, we are going to widen that lens for a bit to see that her story is a part of a much larger one.

We began this study "in the days when the judges ruled."

> **Turn back to the very last verse of Judges and fill in the blank to complete it below:**
>
> **In those days Israel had no _____; everyone did as they saw fit (Judges 21:25).**

Judges is the book just before the Book of Ruth. Now turn to the book of the Bible just after Ruth.

> **What book comes after the Book of Ruth?**

The Book of Ruth falls between Judges and 1 Samuel. Judges is a story about a time when there were no kings. If you glance at the section headings in 1 Samuel, you'll quickly see that it is a story in which God ushers in the first two kings of Israel, Saul and David.

Written by human hands but divinely inspired, Naomi's story is perfectly positioned as a small story in God's much larger story about the history of His people.

The Deeper Story
What does Ruth 4:16-22 tell us about the human characters in this particular narrative?
Does this passage tell us something about God? If so, what does it say?

> Does this passage give us hints that God is at work? If so, what are they?

The Promise We Carry

Today we find another beautiful and unexpected blessing for Naomi. What was empty has now been made full. What was lost has been renewed and renewed abundantly.

The women of Bethlehem, who had heard Naomi's bitter lament when she returned home, now rejoice with her that "Naomi has a son!" (v. 17). The sweetness of God in this gift is almost unbearable. Imagine her delight in the opportunity to share in the joy of a precious baby once more.

> **What details from Naomi's story were likely to make her especially grateful for this gift?**

Extra Insight

Although verses 16-17 imply that Naomi formally adopted Obed, it is more likely these verses are acknowledging that Naomi now has a blood relative to provide and care for her.[10]

When you realize that God is behind every good and perfect gift, the ordinary can become the extraordinary.

Like Naomi, the expected blessing of living with a story that you don't like is that you have an appreciation for what you may have taken for granted before. When you realize that God is behind every good and perfect gift, the ordinary can become the extraordinary. The mundane becomes an everyday miracle.

> **What are some things you are grateful for that many people tend to overlook?**

It would be enough to walk through this broken world with an awareness that every breath you take is a precious gift. But God doesn't leave our stories there.

> **Read the genealogy listed in Ruth 4:18-22.**
>
> **With whom does it start?**
>
> **With whom does it end?**

Naomi's grandson would become the grandfather of King David, one of the greatest kings in the history of Israel. With this knowledge alone, Naomi's story is already a part of a much larger story. But God doesn't stop there.

Turn to the New Testament and read Matthew 1:1-6.

Whose genealogy is listed here?

What names do you recognize in verses 5-6?

Naomi's grandson would become an ancestor of Jesus, the Savior of the world! Can you imagine Naomi sitting face-to-face with Jesus, knowing how her story ended and recounting the moment she changed her name to Mara?

What do you think Jesus would have told Naomi?

I think He might have whispered these words to her:

> ¹*Therefore, since we have so great a cloud of witnesses surrounding us, let us also lay aside every encumbrance and the sin which so easily entangles us, and let us run with endurance the race that is set before us,* ²*fixing our eyes on Jesus, the author and perfecter of faith, who for the joy set before Him endured the cross, despising the shame, and has sat down at the right hand of the throne of God.*

(Hebrews 12:1-2 NASB)

Sister, do you hear Him whispering the same words to you?

Your story is a part of a much larger one and it's time to take your place in it. Your story is a part of Jesus's story. Tucked into the perfect time in history, yours is the gospel story. When you carry a record of sins and mistakes, you carry Jesus's promise for forgiveness. When you carry a story that is broken and beyond repair, you carry Jesus's promise for redemption. When you carry the awareness that your days on earth are numbered, you carry Jesus's promise that your days in eternity with Him are infinite. *When you find hope in trusting Jesus to renew your story, you carry that promise into the hearts of others who need to hear it next.*

Renewed and with hope, may you move forward in strength and courage to bring this good news into the world.

What's Your Story?

So, like Naomi, we will end this story where we began. But I hope we will find that the way we tell our story has changed.

What's your story?

On the timeline below, write the major milestones in your life thus far.

Birth   **Now**

_____

Now take a few moments and describe your story. Has the light appeared, as in Naomi's story? Where has it been marked by blessing? What new truths have enabled you to see God's hand in your story?

Describe the characters in your story. Who has helped shape who you are today?

What is it about your story that you love?

What parts of your story are filled with hope?

The Hope We Will Cling To

There is an abundance of written praise for the literary beauty, poetic story-telling, and rewarding plotline for the Book of Ruth. As we seek to sum up our time in Naomi's story with takeaways that will stay with us long past the closing of this study guide, I want to share one of them with you. It is difficult to choose just one passage, but consider these words from commentator Christopher Ash:

> There is hardly anything in human affairs more devastating than to see a parent burying their son or daughter, and little to rival the birth of a child for bringing us natural joy. The Book of Ruth begins with the former, indeed the death of two sons, and ends with the latter. This story takes us from death to life, from devastation to joy and from despair to hope.[11]

What would you add to this review? How has the Book of Ruth moved you?

Now, flip back through your guide to review the themes we have studied together, and put a star below by the lessons that have resonated most with you.

Theme Review	
Week 1: Ruth 1 **The Story You** **Don't Want**	Difficult stories can become setups for the display of divine strength.
	We can believe in God's sovereignty and still grieve our story.
	The moment our earthly circumstances announce that all is lost is the moment the heavenly seeds of hope are planted.
Week 2: Ruth 2 **The Movement** **You Can't See**	Your details are woven with divine movement, and God is always working for your good.
	Heavenly kindness heals earthly hurts.
	Jesus has the power to redeem both our souls and our stories if we surrender them to Him.
Week 3: Ruth 3 **The Intersection** **of Our Action** **and God's Plan**	When our stories leave us feeling helpless, we can find hope by walking in step with God.
	The hope of God is often delivered through human hands.
	We wait on the Savior to return while we place our hope in Him to renew our story.
Week 4: Ruth 4 **The God Who** **Rescues, Redeems,** **and Renews**	Because of Jesus's sacrifice on the cross, our stories have hope for the future.
	God promises to renew our past, our present, and our future.
	When you find hope in trusting Jesus to renew your story, you carry that promise into the hearts of others who need to hear it next.

Today's Takeaway

When you find hope in trusting Jesus to renew your story, you carry that promise into the hearts of others who need to hear it next.

Closing Prayer

In closing, I offer this prayer adapted for you from the blessing over Naomi in Ruth 4:14-15. Fill in the blanks with your name and lift your renewed voice up to God as you pray.

Praise be to the LORD, who this day has not left _____ without a guardian-redeemer in Jesus. May He become famous throughout all the world! He will renew _____'s life and sustain her in her old age. For He loves _____ and is better to _____ than anything in this entire universe. Amen.

May the God of hope fill you with all joy and peace as you trust in him, so that you may overflow with hope by the power of the Holy Spirit.

(Romans 15:13)

Beloved sister, may you be renewed.

Use the space below to add any extra insights and prayers of your own.

The God Who Rescues, Redeems, and Renews

(Ruth 4)

Welcome/Prayer/Icebreaker (5–10 minutes)

Welcome to Session 4 of *Renewed*! This week we have explored God's redemptive conclusion to Naomi's story as we place our trust in His promise to rescue, redeem, and renew our own stories. We wrapped up our time in the Book of Ruth celebrating with Naomi and clinging to the hope as we take our place in the gospel story. Our time as a group will allow space to dive deeper into questions that arose as you worked through the lessons on your own. Today we will consider how Jesus's sacrifice on the cross brings us hope; how God renews our past, present, and future; and how we bring His hope into the world. Begin by opening up in prayer, and then take a few moments to share one seemingly mundane occurrence that brings you hope.

Video (about 20 minutes)

Play the video segment for Week 4. Just below this section you'll find an outline and space to jot down any notes or extra thoughts you may have while watching the video segment.

—Video Notes—

Scriptures: Romans 15:13; 2 Corinthians 5:17; Isaiah 40:31; Ruth 4:13-17

God rescues our hearts by renewing our _____.

God redeems our stories by replacing them with _____.

God renews our lives by rebuilding our _____.

Other Insights:

Video Discussion

- What does it mean to you to be renewed by God?
- During this study, has God planted renewed hope, purpose, or dreams in your life? If so, share one or more of these with the group.
- What is one way you can share God's promise of renewed hope with others?

Workbook Discussion

- "An unfulfilled dream isn't the end of hope; it might just be the beginning of a new work of God in your life" (Week 4 introduction, page 91). Discuss how you might have seen this manifest in your life.

- How would you define the gospel story?
- On Day 1 (page 96), we read Colossians 1:19-23 and made a list of the costs Jesus incurred for us and the blessings we receive from His redemption. Share one cost and one blessing you listed.
- Describe the ways that God rescued Naomi from her past, present, and future.
- How might the words of Isaiah 49:16 empower us to place our story in God's hands?
- How does the conclusion of this story bring fullness to Naomi's story?
- On Day 3 (page 109), you learned that, "Your story is a part of a much larger one and it's time to take your place in it. Your story is a part of Jesus's story. Tucked into the perfect time in history, yours is the gospel story. When you carry a record of sins and mistakes, you carry Jesus's promise for forgiveness." Describe the feelings that arise when you consider this truth?
- What are you grateful for that most people overlook (Day 3, page 108)?

Finding Hope (10–15 minutes)

Divide into groups of two or three and discuss the following:

- What theme from Naomi's resonated the most with you (Day 3, page 111)?
- What parts of your story has God already redeemed?
- "Renewed and with hope, may you move forward in strength and courage to bring this good news into the world" (Day 3, page 109). Who is one person God might be calling you to share His good news with?

Closing Prayer (5 minutes)

End your group time together by sharing any prayer requests within the group. You may nominate one person to pray for all requests or you may feel comfortable as a group having all members pray together. Ask God to give you the courage to be His storyteller to the world as you wait and hope for Christ's return.

Leader
Helps

Tips for Facilitating a Group

Thank You for Leading

Thank you for investing your time and resources in leading others through the study of God's Word. I know from personal experience that the job is a rewarding one, but I also know it requires an extra layer of thought, prayer, and preparation.

My Bible study leader mentor, MaryAnn, summarizes her role as a facilitator with these three priorities: "open heart, open ears, open home." Open your heart to the work of God in your community through you, open your ears to the needs of those in your group, and open your home (or your church) so women will have a safe and welcoming space to learn about God and study His Word. If you keep these priorities at the forefront of your mind and let God do the rest, I am confident that your group will have a positive and enriching experience with God's Word.

What follows here are tips, resources, and suggestions to help your group get the most out of your time together. The suggestions below are just that, *suggestions*. You will know best how to customize your time based on the needs of the women who are participating in the study.

Much of Jesus's ministry was conducted in a similar way as your group—through a collective experience of talking about God and His Word together in community. This is important work. Know that I am praying for wisdom, discernment, and blessing over you as you encourage women in their faith. Thank you for serving them.

Before the Study Begins

- Pray, pray, pray. Pray for the women attending your study, whether you know their names yet or not. Pray for their families. Pray for yours as you will give of your time to serve your group.
- It is not uncommon for every manner of obstacle to arise for anyone participating in Bible study communities. Be aware of it and pray for protection from any hinderances to learning from God's Word.
- Determine how you will distribute member workbooks. Will you or your church place a bulk order or will you ask each member to secure their own workbook individually?
- Consider how many weeks you will be meeting. It might be beneficial to hold a social gathering before and after the study to allow time for fellowship and building community.

- Consider whether the food will be involved and/or served. If so, how much and who will provide it? Light refreshments? Potluck dinner? Four-course meal? (We can dream, right, girls?) Plan accordingly.
- Think about the technology requirements for hosting the study. You'll need access to a television or other device that can play the teaching videos to the group. If you are watching the teaching segments via DVD, you'll need a DVD player and remote. If you are watching the teaching segments via streaming videos, you'll need working internet service connected to the device you are watching from. (Streaming video files are available at www.Cokesbury.com, or you may access the videos for this study and other Abingdon Women Bible studies on AmplifyMedia.com through an individual or church membership.)
- This seems obvious, but invite women to come! Think of your neighbor, your coworker, your friend you haven't seen in a while. Ask God to place specific people on your heart and to go before you when you invite them to the group.
- If you are hosting the study in your home, block out a few minutes to prepare on the days you are scheduled to meet. It has been my experience that women don't really care if there are cereal on your carpet; what matters most is that your heart is ready to welcome them. Preserving time to get your materials ready and praying for your time together is helpful. Schedule that on your calendar as you can.
- If you have group members with young children and you do not have access to church childcare, consider hiring a babysitter during your time together. Split the cost among the members who will use the childcare.
- Communicate to your group members that they should complete the first week of study lessons on their own before your first meeting. The video teaching segments wrap up what they have already studied individually for each week.

Preparing for the Sessions

- Pray for each group member in attendance, asking God to open their hearts and minds to what He would have everyone learn about His Word. Pray that God's Spirit will guide your discussion and that your conversations would glorify Him. Also, thank Him for the opportunity to serve His kingdom and have a front row seat to watch Him work in the lives of others.
- Consider having nametags if your group is large or includes new faces.
- Before gathering, reread the full chapter of Ruth you will be discussing.
- Collect emails and other contact information from your group. This will be helpful when you want to send some encouraging thoughts or need to change timing or meeting details.

- Communicate logistics and details to your group members so they will know when and where you are meeting.
- Consider gathering a few extra resources each session that might enhance what you are discussing or to encourage those who yearn to go deeper into what they are learning. Some ideas might be a playlist with worship songs that align with your topic, articles related to the discussion, or additional books you can recommend.
- Either print enough Scripture Cards for every person in your group or email a digital copy to them beforehand. Printable Scripture Cards are available at https://therescuedletters.com/renewed.
- Spend a few moments addressing hospitality needs for your meeting space. Make sure there is room for everyone and any additional materials are easily accessible. Extra pens and note-taking supplies are always helpful to have on hand.

Leading the Sessions

- Offer refreshments. They don't have to be fancy. Water and mints or chocolates are always a good option to start with.
- Allow time for introductions and fellowship, letting members catch up with one another. Be mindful of time constraints.
- Go over any announcements that need to be made.
- At your first gathering, ask the group what they are looking forward to most about the study or what drew them to study Ruth. This will help you be sensitive to their needs as you guide them through God's Word.
- At the last gathering, ask the group what resonated with them the most throughout the study. This will help group members connect with one another over shared discoveries and understanding.
- If your group is active on social media, encourage them to use the hashtag #RENEWEDSTUDY to connect with other women doing the study.
- One of the ways you can make your group members feel at ease in group gatherings is to start and end each session on time. Group members are often juggling multiple responsibilities and obligations outside of your meetings, so it's respectful to maintain boundaries on your time together.
- Remind your group members that there is no judgment or shame in not completing the lessons for each week. Ideally, they will have adequate time to complete each lesson because this is where they will make the deepest connections with God's Word. But sometimes life happens, and it's important to extend grace and compassion when obstacles get in the way of our Bible study intentions. Create an environment where they can easily be brought up to speed with the objectives and

discussion topics for each session; the "Group Session Guide Leader Notes" that follow will be particularly helpful with this.

- Remember that you don't have to know all the answers and your group members are not expecting you to be an expert. It's okay to say, "I don't know. Let's see if we can find the answer to that together." The best group leaders provide a welcoming space for learning and discussion while offering structure and guidance for each session.
- If your group is quieter and less talkative, don't be afraid of silence. Be prepared to offer your thoughts on some of the discussion questions to help others feel comfortable with speaking up, but you don't have to fill every minute with talking. Give your members space and freedom to think about what they might want to offer to the discussion.
- Be sensitive to the emotional needs of group members who might have a difficult time processing their thoughts and feelings. Talking about stories that we don't like isn't easy. Offer them a safe space to explore their emotions and remind them that they are not alone.
- Be particularly attentive to members who are joining a group Bible study for the first time. Navigating the Bible can be quite intimidating in a group setting. Don't assume that everyone knows the difference between Bible translations, how to easily locate Scripture references, or that they understand broad theological concepts. Be intentional about making all members feel welcome, included, seen, and heard. Create an environment where group members feel comfortable asking questions.
- If your group is rather chatty, you may have to steer the conversation in order to be mindful of everyone's time. Be aware of the time frames suggested in the "Group Session Guides" and adjust accordingly.
- If you have a member who consistently contributes to the discussion with reflective comments, thought-provoking questions, and extra material resources she has collected before your time together, recognize the possibility that she may have the gift of and interest in teaching. Consider ways to involve her in a leadership role on this and future studies you may participate in together.
- Consider sending prayer requests and supportive comments via email or another form of communication between each session. This can also be a helpful way to encourage group members as they work through their individual lessons.

Materials Needed

- *Renewed* workbook
- *Renewed* DVD and DVD player or access to streaming video segments
- Nametags and markers (optional)
- iPod, smartphone, tablet, and portable speaker (if desired for gathering music)

Group Session Guide Leader Notes

This section gives you a general overview of the study and can be used to help you prepare for each session. You may want to share the main objective and chapter summary with your group members at the beginning of each session, which may be helpful for members who have not had time to complete the individual lessons for the week.

Week 1—The Story You Don't Want

Main Objective

To acknowledge the hard stories we are carrying and that God is in control and can move through what might feel impossible and unchangeable

Scripture Focus

Ruth 1

Chapter Summary

In Ruth 1, we are introduced to Naomi and her family, Israelites who have moved to Moab due to a famine in the land. Naomi's husband is Elimelek; her two sons are named Mahlon and Chilion. Their wives are two Moabite women, Ruth and Orpah. Not long after the story begins, tragedy strikes Naomi's family. Her husband, Elimelek, dies, as do her two sons, leaving Naomi and her daughters-in-law to fend for themselves. After hearing news that God is providing for His people in their hometown of Bethlehem, Naomi decides to return home. Initially, both Ruth and Orpah intend to stay with Naomi, but with some protest from Naomi, Orpah decides to return to her original family in Moab. Ruth, however, is determined to stay with Naomi. So, the two women set out for Bethlehem together. Naomi, bereft with grief over the tragedy that has befallen her family, is overcome with bitterness. Ruth and Naomi arrive in Bethlehem just as the barley harvest is beginning, signaling that hope is on the horizon.

Week 2—The Movement You Can't See

Main Objective

To acknowledge that God is always working in our details, even when we can't see or perceive His movement

Scripture Focus

Ruth 2

Chapter Summary

Naomi and Ruth have arrived in Bethlehem and we learn that there is a relative of Naomi's husband, a man named Boaz. Needing to provide food for themselves, Ruth takes the initiative to find a farm in which she can glean leftover crops. She ends up gleaning from Boaz's farm and the two of them meet. Boaz is an upstanding man whose faith is evident in how he speaks and conducts himself. Boaz extends protection and care to Ruth by instructing her to continue gleaning in his farm and offering water whenever she is thirsty. Ruth is astonished that she would find such favor from Boaz, especially since she is from Moab, and therefore considered a foreigner to the Israelites. Boaz has heard of Ruth's overwhelming kindness to Naomi and he responds with continued generosity and kindness toward Ruth. When Naomi sees the abundant amount of grain Ruth comes home with from Boaz's farm, she reveals that Boaz is one of their guardian-redeemers, a family member who, under the Israelites' law, is obligated to look after Elimelek's survivors and property.

Week 3—The Intersection of Our Action and God's Plan

Main Objective

To acknowledge that God partners with humans to fulfill His plan and bring love and compassion into the world

Scripture Focus

Ruth 3

Chapter Summary

This time it is Naomi's turn to take the initiative. The harvest season is ending and it is time for threshing, which is the process of separating the usable grain from the unusable portions. Motivated by the desire to find Ruth a proper home with a husband who can provide for her, Naomi instructs Ruth to secretly meet with Boaz on the threshing floor. Knowing that Boaz is one of their guardian-redeemers, Naomi hopes that Boaz will offer to marry her. Ruth goes to Boaz on the threshing floor and he does indeed agree to marry her. But he also reveals that there is another guardian-redeemer who is closer in kin to Naomi than he, and therefore would be first in line to redeem Elimelek's property and take care of Naomi and Ruth. Boaz sends Ruth home with a large amount of barley grain, and we are left to wonder what will happen in the morning when Boaz meets with the other guardian-redeemer.

Week 4—The God Who Rescues, Redeems, and Renews

Main Objective

To acknowledge God's promise to rescue us from our grief, redeem our stories, and renew our hearts with joy

Scripture Focus

Ruth 4

Chapter Summary

Boaz meets with the other guardian-redeemer at the town gate, a typical location for conducting business. In front of ten elders as witnesses, he explains Naomi's situation to the other guardian-redeemer and suggests that he purchase the property that belonged to Elimelek. The other guardian-redeemer originally agrees to purchase the property until Boaz tells him that he would also be responsible for Naomi. The other guardian-redeemer declines the opportunity to redeem Elimelek's estate to Boaz, who then announces to the witnesses that he will purchase Elimelek's property and marry Ruth in order to continue Elimelek's name and family line throughout history. The witnesses bless the union and Boaz marries Ruth. They conceive and Ruth gives birth to a son. The women of Bethlehem rejoice with Naomi that God has renewed her life and her story. Naomi helps to raise the son and we learn that he becomes David's grandfather, and therefore an ancestor of Jesus.

Once the Study Is Over

Once the study is over, think of ways to stay connected as a group. Plan a social gathering, have a night reserved just for prayer, or get involved in a service opportunity together. You might even consider attending a women's ministry event as a group or taking a girls' trip together to build community.

If possible, take a few moments to connect with each group member individually. Thank them for studying God's Word with you and make sure they know you value their presence and contribution to the group.

Take time to consider what Bible study you will do next! Hopefully, the group you are leading will continue to walk through God's Word together. As you do, you'll be rewarded with both a precious fulfilling sisterhood and a deepening relationship with your personal Savior.

Your work as a group leader is meaningful and valuable to the kingdom of God and it does not go unnoticed by your heavenly Father. May He bless you richly as you draw women into His Word and move forward in His grace, love, and will.

Video Notes Answers

Week 1
perspective
renewing
bitter

Week 3
outcome
waiting
power / might

Week 2
physical
emotional
spiritual

Week 4
hope
purpose
dreams

Notes

WEEK 1: The Story You Don't Want (Ruth 1)

1. "Contrast: Definitions and Examples," Literary Terms, accessed May 1, 2020, https://literaryterms.net/contrast/.

2. Judy Fentress-Williams, *Abingdon Old Testament Commentaries*: *Ruth*, gen. ed. Patrick D. Miller (Nashville, TN: Abingdon Press, 2012), 37.

3. "Timeline: 3100-1000 BCE," *Oxford Reference* (2012), accessed January 2, 2020, https://www.oxfordreference.com/view/10.1093/acref/9780191735363.timeline.0001.

4. Gordon D. Fee and Douglas Stuart, *How to Read the Bible for All Its Worth*: *A Guide to Understanding the Bible*, 2nd ed. (Grand Rapids, MI: Zondervan, 1993), 89.

5. Fentress-Williams, *Ruth*, 40.

6. Ann Spangler and Jean E. Syswerda, *Women of the Bible*: *A One-Year Devotional Study of Women in Scripture* (Grand Rapids, MI: Zondervan Publishing House, 1999), 131.

7. Kenneth C. Way, *Judges and Ruth*, Teach the Text Commentary Series, gen. eds. John H. Walton (Old Testament) and Mark L. Strauss (New Testament) (Grand Rapids, MI: Baker Books, a division of Baker Publishing Group, 2016), 188.

8. "How Should the Different Genres of the Bible Impact How We Interpret the Bible?," Got Questions Ministries, accessed May 1, 2020, https://www.gotquestions.org/Bible-genres.html.

9. Fee and Stuart, *How to Read the Bible for All Its Worth*, 78–79.

10. Fee and Stuart. *How to Read the Bible for All Its Worth*, 78.

11. Magic Tree House, accessed January 2, 2020, https://www.magictreehouse.com/books/.

12. Christopher Ash, *Teaching Ruth and Esther*: *From Text to Message*, Proclamation Trust's Teaching the Bible Series, eds. David Jackman and Jon Gemmell (Fearn, Ross-shire, Scotland: Christian Focus Publications, 2018), 46–47.

13. Stephen J. Wellum, "Covenants," in *Holman Illustrated Bible Dictionary*, *Revised and Expanded*, gen. ed. Chad Brand (Nashville, TN: B&H Publishing Group, 2015), 358.

14. Ash, *Teaching Ruth and Esther*, 53.

15. Adele Berlin, *Poetics and Interpretation of Biblical Narrative* (1983; repr., Winona Lake, IN: Eisenbrauns, 2005), 103.

16. Berlin, *Poetics and Interpretation of Biblical Narrative*, 104.

17. Way, *Judges and Ruth*, 188.

18. John W. Reed, "Ruth," in *The Bible Knowledge Commentary*: *Old Testament*, Bible Knowledge Commentary Series, gen. eds. John F. Walvoord and Roy B. Zuck (Colorado Springs, CO: David C. Cook, 1985), 420.

19. Warren W. Wiersbe, *Be Committed*: *Doing God's Will Whatever the Cost*, The BE Series Commentary on Ruth and Esther, 2nd ed. (Victory Books, 1993; Colorado Springs, CO: David C. Cook, 2008), 23–24; Daniel Isaac Block, *Judges, Ruth*, The New American Commentary, gen. ed. E. Ray Clendenen (Nashville, TN: Broadman & Holman, 1999), 637, 639.

20. Ash, *Teaching Ruth and Esther*, 54; Robert L. Hubbard Jr., *The Book of Ruth*, The New International Commentary on the Old Testament Series (Grand Rapids, MI: Wm. B. Eerdmans, 1988), 113; Reed, "Ruth," in *The Bible Knowledge Commentary*: *Old Testament*, 420.

21. Sharon Dirckx, "Why Grief Is Evidence for God," The Gospel Coalition, May 10, 2016, https://www .thegospelcoalition.org/article/why-grief-is-evidence-for-god/.

22. Wiersbe, *Be Committed*, 23.

23. Hubbard Jr., *The Book of Ruth*, 113.

24. T. Preston Pearce, "Sovereignty of God," in *Holman Illustrated Bible Dictionary, Revised and Expanded*, 1494.

25. Way, *Judges and Ruth*, 188.

26. Fentress-Williams, *Ruth*, 40.

27. Mary J. Evans, *Judges and Ruth: An Introduction and Commentary*, Tyndale Old Testament Commentaries, series ed. David G. Firth (Downers Grove, IL: InterVarsity Press, 2017), 247.

28. Fentress-Williams, *Ruth*, 62.

29. Hubbard Jr., *The Book of Ruth*, 130.

WEEK 2: The Movement You Can't See (Ruth 2)

1. Strong's Greek 3874, s.v. paraklésis: a calling to one's aid, i.e. encouragement, comfort. *Strong's Concordance*, BibleHub.com, accessed April 29, 2020, https://biblehub.com/greek/3874.htm.

2. Strong's Greek 3870, s.v. parakaleó: to call to or for, to exhort, to encourage. *Strong's Concordance*, BibleHub.com, accessed April 29, 2020, https://biblehub.com/greek/3870.htm.

3. Strong's Hebrew 5162, s.v. nacham: to be sorry, console oneself. *Strong's Concordance*, BibleHub.com, accessed April 29, 2020, https://biblehub.com/hebrew/5162.htm.

4. "What Is the Gift of Encouragement?," Got Questions Ministries, accessed May 1, 2020, https://www .gotquestions.org/gift-of-encouragement.html.

5. Fentress-Williams, *Ruth*, 65.

6. Reed, "Ruth," in *The Bible Knowledge Commentary: Old Testament*, 422.

7. Hubbard Jr., *The Book of Ruth*, 138.

8. Way, *Judges and Ruth*, 195.

9. Way, *Judges and Ruth*, 198.

10. Ash, *Teaching Ruth and Esther*, 75.

11. "The Science of Kindness," Random Acts of Kindness, accessed January 7, 2020, https://www .randomactsofkindness.org/the-science-of-kindness.

12. Way, *Judges and Ruth*, 196.

13. Way, *Judges and Ruth*, 203.

14. Ash, *Teaching Ruth and Esther*, 81.

15. Ash, *Teaching Ruth and Esther*, 81.

16. Stan Norman, "Redeem, Redemption, Redeemer," in *Holman Illustrated Bible Dictionary, Revised and Expanded*, 1339.

WEEK 3: The Intersection of Our Action and God's Plan (Ruth 3)

1. Way, *Judges and Ruth*, 201–202.

2. Paraphrase of Way, *Judges and Ruth*, 201–202.

3.   Reed, "Ruth," in *The Bible Knowledge Commentary: Old Testament*, 424.
4.   Way, *Judges and Ruth*, 202.
5.   Reed, "Ruth," in *The Bible Knowledge Commentary: Old Testament*, 424.
6.   Ash, *Teaching Ruth and Esther*, 94.
7.   Hubbard Jr., *The Book of Ruth*, 200.
8.   Way, *Judges and Ruth*, 202.
9.   Way, *Judges and Ruth*, 205.
10. Ash, *Teaching Ruth and Esther*, 99.
11. Ash, *Teaching Ruth and Esther*, 77.
12. Way, *Judges and Ruth*, 203.
13. Ash, *Teaching Ruth and Esther*, 106. See also Strong's Hebrew 7387, s.v. reqam: emptily, vainly. *Strong's Concordance*, BibleHub.com, accessed April 30, 2020, https://biblehub.com/hebrew/7387.htm.
14. Fentress-Williams, *Ruth*, 104.
15. Hubbard Jr., *The Book of Ruth*, 226–227.

WEEK 4: The God Who Rescues, Redeems, and Renews (Ruth 4)

1.   Ash, *Teaching Ruth and Esther*, 114.
2.   Way, *Judges and Ruth*, 209.
3.   Ash, *Teaching Ruth and Esther*, 115.
4.   Ash, *Teaching Ruth and Esther*, 114.
5.   Evans, *Judges and Ruth: An Introduction and Commentary*, 265.
6.   Ash, *Teaching Ruth and Esther*, 117.
7.   Ash, *Teaching Ruth and Esther*, 118.
8.   Ash, *Teaching Ruth and Esther*, 119.
9.   Mitchell L. Chase, "A True and Greater Boaz: Typology and Jesus in the Book of Ruth," *The Southern Baptist Journal of Theology* 21, no. 1 (Spring 2017): https://equip.sbts.edu/publications/journals/journal-of-theology/sbjt-211-spring-2017/true-greater-boaz-typology-jesus-book-ruth/.
10. Hubbard Jr., *The Book of Ruth*, 274.
11. Ash, *Teaching Ruth and Esther*, 127.